Darkest India

Commissioner Booth-Tucker

Contents

PREFACE. 7

PART I.--IN DARKEST INDIA. 10

CHAPTER I. WHY "DARKEST INDIA?" 10

CHAPTER II. WHO ARE NOT THE SUBMERGED TENTH?........................ 12

CHAPTER III. THE MINIMUM STANDARD OF EXISTENCE.................... 14

CHAPTER IV. WHO ARE THE SUBMERGED TENTH?......................... 18

CHAPTER V. THE BEGGARS. 21

CHAPTER VI. "THE OUT-OF-WORKS." 25

CHAPTER VII. THE HOMELESS POOR. 28

CHAPTER VIII. THE LAND OF DEBT. 31

CHAPTER IX. THE LAND OF FAMINE. 33

CHAPTER X. THE LAND OF PESTILENCES. 36

CHAPTER XI. THE WHITE ANTS OF INDIAN SOCIETY. 39

CHAPTER XII. THE CRIMINALS.. 44

CHAPTER XIII. ON THE BORDER LAND. 49

CHAPTER XIV.ELEMENTS OF HOPE. 52

PART II.--THE WAY OUT.. 55

CHAPTER I. THE ESSENTIALS TO SUCCESS. 55

CHAPTER II. WHAT IS GENERAL BOOTH'S SCHEME?.......................... 57

CHAPTER III. THE CITY COLONY.. 59

CHAPTER IV. THE LABOR BUREAU. 61

CHAPTER V. FOOD FOR ALL--THE FOOD DEPOTS............................... 65

CHAPTER VI. WORK FOR ALL, OR THE LABOUR YARD. 67

CHAPTER VII. SHELTER FOR ALL, OR THE HOUSING OF THE DESTITUTE. 72

CHAPTER VIII. THE BEGGARS BRIGADE. 74

CHAPTER IX. THE PRISON GATE BRIGADE... 83

CHAPTER X. THE DRUNKARD'S BRIGADE. 92

CHAPTER XI. THE RESCUE HOMES FOR THE FALLEN........................... 93

CHAPTER XII. "THE COUNTRY COLONY"--"WASTEWARD HO!" 94

CHAPTER XIII. THE SUBURBAN FARM.. 98

CHAPTER XIV. THE INDUSTRIAL VILLAGE... 100

CHAPTER XV. THE SOCIAL TERRITORY, OR, POOR MAN'S PARADISE.............. 103

CHAPTER XVI. THE SOCIAL CITY OF REFUGE. 110

CHAPTER XVII. SUPPLEMENTARY BRANCHES OF THE COUNTRY COLONY. .. 113

CHAPTER XVIII. THE OVER-SEA COLONY. 116

CHAPTER XIX MISCELLANEOUS AGENCIES. 119

CHAPTER XX. HOW MUCH WILL IT COST? 121

CHAPTER XXI. A PRACTICAL CONCLUSION.. 125

APPENDIX.. 128

DARKEST INDIA

BY

Commissioner Booth-Tucker

PREFACE.

The remarkable reception accorded to General Booth's "In Darkest England and the Way Out," makes it hardly necessary for me to apologise for the publication of the following pages, which are intended solely as an introduction to that fascinating book, and in order to point out to Indian readers that if a "cabhorse charter" is both desirable and practicable for England (see page 19, Darkest England) a "bullock charter" is no less urgently needed for India.

In doing this it is true that certain modifications and adaptations in detail will require to be made. But the more carefully I consider the matter, the more convinced do I become, that these will be of an unimportant character and that the gospel of social salvation, which has so electrified all classes in England, can be adopted in this country almost as it stands.

After all, this is no new gospel, but simply a resurrection, or resuscitation, of a too much neglected aspect of the original message of "peace on earth, good will towards men," proclaimed at Bethlehem. It has been the glory of Christianity, that it has in all ages and climes acknowledged the universal brotherhood of man, and sought to relieve the temporal as well as the spiritual needs of the masses. Of late years that glory has in some degree departed, or at least been tarnished, not because the efforts put forth are less than those in any previous generation, but because the need is so far greater, that what would have been amply sufficient a few centuries ago, is altogether inadequate when compared to the present great necessity.

The very magnitude of the problem has struck despair into the hearts of would-be reformers, many of whom have leapt to the conclusion, that nothing but an entire reconstruction of society could cope with so vast an evil, whilst others have been satisfied with simply putting off the reckoning day and suppressing the simmering volcano on the edge of which, they dwelt with paper edicts which its first fierce eruption is destined to consume.

Surely the present plan if at all feasible, is God-inspired, and if God-inspired, it will be certainly feasible. And surely of all countries under the face of the sun there is none which more urgently needs the proclamation of some such Gospel of Hope than does India. That it is both needed and feasible I trust that in the following pages I shall be able to abundantly prove.

General Booth has uttered a trumpet-call, the echoes of which will be reverberated through the entire world. The destitute masses, whom he has in his book so vividly pourtrayed, are everywhere to be found. And I believe I speak truly when I say that in no country is their existence more palpable, their number more numerous, their misery more aggravated, their situation more critical, desperate and devoid of any gleam of hope to relieve their darkness of despair, than in India.

And yet perhaps in no country is there so promising a sphere for the inauguration of General Booth's plan of campaign. Religious by instinct, obedient to discipline, skilled in handicrafts, inured to hardship, and accustomed to support life on the scantiest conceivable pittance, we cannot imagine a more fitting object for our pity, nor a more encouraging one for our effort, than the members of India's "submerged tenth."

Leaving to the care of existing agencies those whose bodies are diseased, General Booth's scheme seeks to fling the mantle of brotherhood around the morally sick, the destitute and the despairing. It seeks to throw the bridge of love and hope across the growing bottomless abyss in which are struggling twenty-six millions of our fellow men, whose sin is their misfortune and whose poverty is their crime, who are graphically said to have been "damned into the world, rather than born into it."

The question is a national one. This is no time therefore for party or sectarian feeling to be allowed to influence our minds. True for ourselves we still believe as fully as ever that the salvation of Jesus Christ is the one great panacea for all the sins and miseries of mankind. True we are still convinced that to merely improve a man's circumstances without changing the man himself will be largely labor spent in vain. True we believe in a hell and in a Heaven, and that it is our ultimate object to save each individual whom we can influence out of the one into the other. True that among the readers of the following pages will be those whose religious creed differs from our's as widely as does the North Pole from the South.

But about these matters let us agree for the present to differ. Let us unite with hand and heart to launch forthwith the social life boat, and let us commit it to the waves, which are every moment engulfing the human wrecks with which our shores are lined. When the tempest has ceased to rage, and when the last dripping mariner has been safely landed we can, if we wish, with a peaceful conscience dissolve our partnership and renew the discussion of the minor differences, which divide, distract and weaken the human race, but *not till then.*

PART I.--IN DARKEST INDIA.

CHAPTER I.
WHY "DARKEST INDIA?"

I t is unnecessary for me to recapitulate the parallel drawn by General Booth between the sombre, impenetrable and never-ending forest, discovered by Stanley in the heart of Africa, and the more fearfully tangled mass of human corruption to be found in England. Neither the existence, nor the extent, of the latter have been called in question, and in reckoning the submerged at one tenth of the entire population it is generally admitted that their numbers have been understated rather than otherwise.

Supposing that a similar percentage be allowed for India, we are face to face with the awful fact that the "submerged tenth" consists of no less than *twenty-six millions of human beings*, who are in a state of destitution bordering upon absolute starvation! No less an authority than Sir William Hunter has estimated their numbers at fifty millions, and practically his testimony remains unimpeached.

Indeed I have heard it confidently stated by those who are in a good position to form a judgement, that at least one hundred millions of the population of India scarcely ever know from year's end to year's end what it is to have a satisfying meal, and that it is the rule and not the exception for them to retire to rest night after night hungry and faint for want of sufficient and suitable food.

I am not going, however to argue in favor of so enormous a percentage of destitution. I would rather believe, at any rate for the time being, that such an estimate is considerably exaggerated. Yet do what we will, it is impossible for any one who has lived in such close and constant contact with the poor, as we have been doing for the last eight or nine years, to blink the fact, that destitution of a most painful character exists, to a very serious extent, even when harvests are favorable and the country is not desolated by the scourge of famine.

Nor do I think that there would be much difficulty in proving that this submerged mass constitutes at least one-tenth of the entire population. No effort has hitherto been made to gauge their numbers, so that it is impossible to speak with accuracy, and the best that we can do is, to form the nearest feasible estimate from the various facts which lie to hand and which are universally admitted.

Let any one who is tempted to doubt the literal truth of what I say, or to think that the picture is overdrawn, but place himself at our disposal for a few days, or weeks, and we will undertake to show him, and that in districts which are as the very Paradise of India, thousands of cases of chronic destitution (especially at certain seasons in the year) such as ought to be sufficient to melt even a heart of stone!

CHAPTER II.
WHO ARE NOT THE SUBMERGED TENTH?

Before passing on to consider of whom the destitute classes actually consist, it will be well in a country like India to make a few preliminary remarks regarding the numbers and position of their more fortunate countrymen who have employment of some sort, and are therefore excluded from the category.

The entire population of British India, including Ceylon, Burmah, and the Native States amounts according to the Census of 1881 to about two hundred and sixty-four millions.

These I would divide into five classes--

1st--The wealth and aristocracy of the country consisting of those who enjoy a monthly income of one hundred rupees and upwards per family. According to the most sanguine estimate we can hardly suppose that these would number more than forty millions of the population.

2nd.--The well-to-do middle classes, earning twenty rupees and upwards, numbering say seventy millions.

3rd.--The fairly well off laboring classes, whose wages are from five rupees and upwards, numbering say at the most one hundred millions.

4th--The poverty stricken laboring classes, earning less than five rupees a month for the support of their families. These cannot at the lowest estimate be less than twenty-five millions.

5th.--The destitute and unemployed poor, who earn nothing at all, and who are dependent for their livelihood on the charity of others. These can hardly be less than twenty-five millions, or a little less than one-tenth of the entire population.

The two hundred and ten millions who are supposed to be earning regularly from five rupees and upwards per family, we may dismiss forthwith from consideration. For the time being they are beyond the reach of want, and they are not therefore the objects of our solicitude. At some future date it may be possible to consider schemes for their amelioration.

Indirectly, no doubt, they will benefit immensely by any plans that will relieve them of the dead weight of twenty-five million paupers, hanging round their necks and crippling their resources. But for the present we may say in regard to them, happy is the man who can reckon upon a regular income of five rupees a month for the support of himself and his family, albeit he may have two or three relations dependent on him, and a capricious money lender ever on his track, ready to extort a lion's share of his scanty earnings. And thrice happy is the man who can boast an income of ten, fifteen, or twenty rupees a month, though the poorest and least skilled laborers in England would reckon themselves badly paid on as much per week.

We turn from these to the workless tenth and to the other tenth who eke out a scanty hand-to-mouth existence on the borders of that great and terrible wilderness. But before enumerating and classifying them, there is one other important question which calls for our consideration.

CHAPTER III.
THE MINIMUM STANDARD OF EXISTENCE.

What may reasonably be said to be the minimum scale of existence, below which no Indian should be suffered to descend? Fix it as low as you like, and you will unfortunately find that there are literally *millions* who do not come up to your standard.

Pick out your coarsest, cheapest grains, and weigh them to the last fraction of an ounce. Rigidly exclude from the poor man's bill of fare any of the relishes which he so much esteems, and the cost of which is so insignificant as to be hardly worth mentioning, and yet you will find legions of gaunt, hungry men, women and children, who would greedily accept your offered regimen to-morrow, if you could only discover the wherewithal for obtaining the same, and who would gladly *pay for it with the hardest and most disagreeable description of labour.*

Take for instance the prison diet, where the food is given by weight, and where it is purposely of the coarsest description consistent with health. That the quantity is insufficient to satisfy the cravings of hunger I can myself testify, having spent a month inside one of Her Majesty's best appointed Bombay prisons, and having noted with painful surprise the eagerness with which every scrap of my own coarse brown bread, that I might leave over, was claimed and eaten by some of my hungry, low-caste fellow prisoners!

The clothing and the blankets are also of the very cheapest description. Of course it must be remembered too, that the food and materials being bought in large quantities, are obtained at contract prices which are considerably less than the usual retail rates in the bazaar. And yet notwithstanding these facts it costs the Bombay Government on an average Rs. 2/4 per month for each prisoner's food, and close upon Rs. 2 a year for clothing, besides the cost of establishment, police guard, hospital expenses and contingencies. Altogether according to the figures given in the Jail Report of 1887 for the Bombay Presidency, including all the above mentioned items, I find that the average monthly cost to Government for each prisoner is a little over Rs. 6 a head.

Now it is a notorious, though almost incredible, fact, that in many parts of India, men will commit petty thefts and offences on purpose to be sent to jail, and will candidly state this to be their reason for doing so. Many Government Officials will, I am sure, bear me out in this. Here we have men who are positively so destitute that they are not only prepared to accept with thankfulness the scanty rations of a jail, but are willing to sacrifice their characters and endure the ignominy of imprisonment and the consequent loss of liberty and separation from home and family, because there is absolutely no other way of escape! In Ceylon the jail is familiarly known among this class as their "Loku amma", or "Grandmother"!

India has no poor law. There is not even the inhospitable shelter of a workhouse, to which the honest pauper may have recourse. Hence with tens of thousands it is literally a case of "steal or starve." I suppose that nine-tenths of the thefts and robberies, besides a large proposition of the other crimes committed in India, are prompted by sheer starvation, and until the cause be removed, it will be in vain to look for a diminution of the evil, multiply our police and soldiery as we will.

But I am digressing. My special object in this chapter is to show the minimum amount which is necessary for the subsistence of our destitute classes.

Another very interesting indication of the minimum cost of living in the cheapest native style, consistent with health, and a very moderate degree of comfort, is furnished by the experience of our village officers to whom we make a subsistence allowance of from eight to twelve annas per week. This with the local gifts of food which they collect in the village enables them to live in the simplest way, and ensures them at least one good meal of curry and rice daily, the rest being locally supplied.

Here is the account of one of our Native Captains as to how he used to manage with his allowance of eight annas a week. I have taken it down myself from his own lips.

"When in charge of a village corps, I received with others my weekly allowance. When I was alone I used to get 10 annas, and when there were two of us together we got eight annas each. This was sufficient to give us one good meal of kheechhree (rice and dal) every day, with a little over for extras, such as firewood, vegetables, oil and ghee.

"We had two regular cooked meals daily, one about noon and the other in the evening. Besides this we also had a piece of bajari bread left over from the previous day, when we got up in the morning.

"For the morning meal we used to beg once a week uncooked food from the villagers. They gave us about eight or nine seers, enough to last us for the week.

"It was a mixture of grains, consisting ordinarily of bajari, bhavtu, kodri, jawar and mat. These we got ground up into flour. It made a sort of bread which is known as Sangru and which we liked very much. With it we would take some sag (vegetables) or dal. This was our regular midday meal.

"Including the value of the food we begged, the cost of living was just about two annas a day for each of us. We could live comfortably upon this.

"The poorer Dhers in the villages seldom or never get kheechhree (rice and dal). They could not afford it. Most of them live on "ghens" (a mixture of buttermilk and coarse flour cooked into a sort of skilly, or gruel) and bhavtu or bajari bread, or "Sangru." The buttermilk is given to them by the village landowners, in return for their labour. They are expected for instance to do odd jobs, cut grass, carry wood, &c. The grain they commonly get either in harvest time in return for labour, or buy it as they require it several maunds at a time. Occasionally they get it in exchange for cloth.

Living in the cheapest possible way, and eating the coarsest food, I
don't think they could manage on less than one annas' worth of food
a day."

One of our European Officers, Staff Captain Hunter, who has lived in the same
style for about four years among the villagers of Goojarat, and who has been in
charge of some 30 or 40 of our Officers, confirms the above particulars. He says
that on two annas a day it is possible to live comfortably, but that one anna is the
minimum below which it is impossible to go in order to support life even on the
coarsest sorts of food.

He tells me that the weavers have assured him that when husband and wife
are working hard from early to late, they cannot make more than four annas profit
a day by their weaving, since the mills have come into the country and then they
have to pay a commission to some one to sell their cloth for them, or spend a considerable time travelling about the country finding a market for it themselves. A piece
of cloth which would fetch nine rupees a few years ago, is now only worth three
and a half or four rupees.

Bearing in mind, therefore, the above facts, I should consider that if India's
submerged tenth are to be granted, even nothing better than a "bullock charter,"
the lowest fraction which could be named for the minimum claimable by all would
be one anna a day, or two rupees a month for each adult. As a matter of fact, I have
no hesitation in saying, that there are many millions in India who do not get even
half this pittance from year's end to year's end, and yet toil on with scarcely a mur-
mur, sharing their scanty morsel with those even poorer than themselves, until
disease finds their weakened bodies an easy prey, and death gives them their release
from a poverty-stricken existence; which scarcely deserves the name of "life."

CHAPTER IV.
WHO ARE THE SUBMERGED TENTH?

By classifying and grading the various orders that constitute Indian Society according to their average earnings, and by considering their minimum, standard of existence, I have sought to prepare the way for a more careful investigation of those who actually constitute the Darkest India, which we are seeking to describe. I have narrowed down our inquiry to the fifty millions, or whatever may be their number, who are either absolutely destitute, or so closely on the border-land of starvation as to need our immediate sympathy and assistance.

Strictly speaking it is with the former alone, the absolutely destitute, numbering as I have supposed some twenty-five millions, that we are at present concerned. I have, however, found it impossible to exclude some reference to the poverty-stricken laboring classes, earning less than five rupees a month for the support of each family, inasmuch as they are probably far more numerous than I have supposed, and their miseries are but one degree removed from those of the utterly destitute. Indeed we scarcely know which is the most to be pitied, the beggar who, if he has nothing, has perhaps at least the comfort that nobody is dependent on him, or the poor coolie who with his three or four rupees a month has from five to eight, or more, mouths to fill! *Fill* did I say? They are *never* filled! The most that can be done in such cases is to prolong life and to keep actual starvation at bay, and that only it may be for a time!

Nevertheless, I have restricted the term "Submerged Tenth" to the absolutely destitute, whom I now proceed to still further analyse.

In doing so I have been obliged to include several important classes who happily do not exist in England, or who are at any rate so few in number, or so well provided for, as not to merit special attention. I mean the beggars, the destitute debtors, and the victims of opium, famine, and pestilence, without whom our catalogue would certainly be incomplete.

Including the above we may say that the Indian Submerged Tenth consist of the following classes:--

I. The Beggars, excluding religious mendicants.

II. The out-of-works,--the destitute, but honest, poor, who are willing and anxious for employment, but unable to obtain it.

III. The Houseless Poor.

IV. The Destitute Debtors.

V. The Victims of Famine and Scarcity.

VI. The Victims of Pestilence.

VII. The Vicious, including

(a) Drunkards.

(b) Opium eaters.

(c) Prostitutes.

VIII. The Criminals, or those who support themselves by crime.

They are alike in one respect, that if they were compelled to be solely dependent upon the proceeds of their labor, it would be impossible for them to exist for a single month.

It is these who constitute the problem which we are endeavouring to solve. Here is the leprous spot of society on which we desire to place our finger. If any think, that it is not so big as we imagine, we will not quarrel with them about its size. Let them cut down our figures to half the amount we have supposed. It will still be large enough to answer the purpose of this inquiry, and should surely serve to arrest the attention of the most callous and indifferent! About its existence no one can have the smallest doubt, nor as to the serious nature of the plague which afflicts our society. As to the character of the remedy, there may be a thousand different opinions but that a remedy is called for, who can question?

CHAPTER V.
THE BEGGARS.

One of the chief problems of Indian Society is that of beggary. India is perhaps the most beggar-beridden country to be found. Nor would it be possible under present circumstances to pass any law forbidding beggary. In the absence of a poor-law, it is the last resource of the destitute.

True it is a plague spot in society and a serious reflection both on our humanity and civilisation, to say nothing of our religious professions, to tolerate the continued existence of the present state of things.

And yet I see no reason why the problem should not be firmly and successfully handled in the interests alike of the beggars themselves and those who supply the alms.

A short time ago I was visiting a Mahommedan gentleman in the Native quarter of Bombay. It was in the morning before he went to business, and I happened to hit upon the very time when the beggars made their usual rounds. I should think upwards of fifty men and women must have called during the few minutes that I was there. In fact it seemed like one never-ending string of them reaching down both sides of the street. Some sang, or shouted, to attract notice; others stood mutely with appealing eyes, wherever they thought there was a chance of getting anything. Many received a dole, while others were told to call again. I could not but be struck by the courteous manner of my host to them, even when asking them to pass along.

On the opposite side of the road some food, or money, I forget which, was being distributed to a hungry crowd by another hospitable merchant. Evidently the supply was limited, and it was a case of first come first served. The desperate struggle that was going on amongst that little crowd of some fifty or sixty people was pitiful to behold.

Now the present system, while better than nothing, is fraught with many serious objections, with which I am sure my Indian readers will agree.

1. The weakest must inevitably go to the wall. It is the strong able-bodied lusty beggar who is bound to get the best of it in struggles such as I have above described, although he is just the one who could and ought to work and who least needs the charity. He is able also to cover more ground than the weak and sickly. To the latter the struggle for existence is necessarily very severe, and while needing and deserving help the most they get the least.

2. This unsystematic haphazard mode of helping the poor is bound to be attended with serious inequalities; while some get more than is either good, or necessary, others get too little, and for the majority even supposing that on two or three days of the week they succeeded in getting a sufficiency, the chances are that on four or five they would not get nearly enough. It would be interesting to know the total amount of food thus distributed and the number of mouths that claim a share.

3. Of course in the case of any rise in the price of grains, the position of the beggar is specially painful, as it is upon him that the weight of the scarcity first falls.

4. Again the present system is a distinct encouragement to fraud. It is impossible for the givers of charity to know anything about the characters of those to whom they give. Thus much of their generosity is misapplied, and the most pitiable cases escape notice, either because they have not so plausible a tale, or because they have not the requisite "cheek" for pushing their claims.

5. While the generous are severely taxed, the less liberal get off scot free. They cannot give to all and therefore they will give to nobody. Some beggars are frauds, therefore they will help none. They have been taken in once, therefore they do not mean to be taken in again.

6. Finally the Indian army of beggars is continually increasing, and will sooner or later have to be dealt with. Private charity will soon be unable to cope with its demands, and humanity forbids that we should leave them to starve.

I return therefore to the question, can we not seize this opportunity, in the common interests of both beggars and be-begged, for dealing vigorously with the difficulty, and for mitigating it, if we cannot at one stroke entirely remove it?

I am very hopeful that this can be done, and that now certain classes of beggars. But in any case I think we may fairly view the problem in a spirit of hopefulness.

Roughly speaking the beggars may be divided into four classes:--

(a) The blind and the infirm.

(b) Those who take them about and share the proceeds of their begging.

(c) The able bodied out-of-works, and

(d) The religious mendicants.

Passing over the last of these for obvious reasons, I would confine myself to the first three classes. But I must not anticipate. The scheme for their deliverance is fully described in a later portion of this book, and for the present I would only say that they constitute a very important section of India's submerged tenth and no plan would be perfect that did not take them fully into account.

It is true that this does not form a part of General Booth's original scheme. But the reason for this is patent. In England vagrancy is forbidden. There is a poor law in operation and there are work-houses provided by the State. In India there is nothing of the kind, save a law for the ***compulsory emigration*** of European va-grants, who are deported by Government and not allowed to return. For Natives there is no choice save the grim one between ***beggary, starvation,*** and ***the jail.*** To obtain the shelter of the last of these they must leave their family, sacrifice their liberty, and commit some offence. Therefore the honest out-of-works are driven by tens of thousands to lives of beggary, which too often pave the way for lives of imposture and crime.

That the problem is capable of being successfully solved, if wisely handled, has been proved by the Bavarian experiment of Count Rumford quoted by General Booth in an appendix to his book. True that in that case the Government lent their authority, their influence and the public purse to the carrying out of the Count's plan of campaign.

This we do not think that public opinion would permit of in India, even if Government should be willing to undertake so onerous a responsibility. Nor do I believe that there is any necessity for it. The circumstances are a good deal different to those in Bavaria, and will be better met by the proposals which I have elsewhere drawn up.

Anyhow it is high time that something should be done, and that on an exten-sive scale and of such a drastic nature as to deal effectually with the question.

I can easily imagine that some may fear lest in dealing with the system we should wound the religious susceptibilities of the people. Begging has come to be such a national institution and is so much a part and parcel of the Indian's life and religion, that any proposal to extinguish the fraternity may cause in some minds positive regret. To such I would say that we do not propose to ***extinguish*** but to ***re-form***, and with this one hint I must beg them, before making up their minds, to study carefully the proposals detailed in Chapter VII of Part II.

CHAPTER VI.
"THE OUT-OF-WORKS."

I should question whether there is a single town or country district in India which does not present the sad spectacle of a large number of men, willing and anxious to work, but unable to find employment. Moreover, as is well known, they have almost without exception families dependent upon them for their support, who are necessarily the sharers of their misfortunes and sufferings. There is one district in Ceylon, where deaths from starvation have been personally known to our Officers, and yet the country appears to be a very garden of Eden for beauty and fertility.

In the early years of our work I remember begging food from a house, and learning afterwards that what they had given us was positively the last they had for their own use. Needless to say that it was hastily returned. During the same visit a cry of "Thief, thief!" was raised in the night. We learnt next morning that the robbery had been committed by a man whose wife and child were starving. It consisted of rice, and the thief was discovered partly by the disappearance of the suspected person, and partly by the fact that in his house was found the exact quantity which had been stolen, whereas it was known that on the previous day he had absolutely nothing whatever in his house! He had left it all for his starving wife and child, and had himself fled to another part of the country, probably going to swell the number of criminals or mendicants in some adjoining city.

I quote these instances as serving to show the impossibility of judging merely from outside appearances in regard to the existence or non-existence of destitution of the most painful character, which it is often to the interest of the local landlords to whitewash and conceal. It is only on looking under the surface that such can in many cases be discovered. It has been the actual living among the people that has made it possible for us to obtain glimpses of their home life, such as could not otherwise have been the case.

But let me enumerate a few of the classes among whom the Indian "Out-of-works" are to be found. I do not mean of course to imply that the entire castes, or tribes, or professions, referred to, constitute them. Far from it. A large proportion are comparatively well off, and though entangled almost universally in debt, are included among the 210 millions with whom we are not now concerned. None the less it will be admitted, I believe, that it is from these that the ranks of destitution are chiefly recruited. I call attention to this fact, because it helps in a large measure to remove the religious difficulty which might at first sight appear likely to stand in the way of our being commissioned by the Indian public to undertake these much-needed reforms. They are almost without exception of either no caste, or of such low caste, that religiously speaking they may justly be regarded as "no man's land." The higher castes and the respectable classes are mostly able to look after themselves, and will not therefore come within the scope of our scheme.

And yet on the threshold of our inquiry we are confronted with an important and increasing class, of "out-of-works" who are being turned out of our educational establishments, unfitted for a life of hard labour, trained for desk service, but without any prospect of suitable employment in the case of a great and continually increasing majority. I do not see how it will be possible for us to exclude or ignore this class in our regimentation of the unemployed. Certainly our sympathies go out very greatly after them. But beyond registering them in our labour bureau, and acting as go-betweens in finding employment for a small fraction of them, I do not see what more can be done. However, the majority of them have well-to-do relations and friends to whom they can turn, and except in cases of absolute destitution will not fall within the scope of the present effort.

Passing over these we come to the poorest classes of peasant proprietors who, having mortgaged their tiny allotments to the hilt, have finally been sold up by the money-lender. Add to these again the more respectable sections of day-laborers. Then there are the destitute among the weavers, tanners, sweepers and other portions of what constitute the low-caste community. Out of these take now the case of the weaver caste, with whom we happen to be particularly familiar, as our work in Gujarat is largely carried on among them. Since the introduction of machinery, their lot has come to be particularly pitiable. In one district it is reckoned that there are 400,000 of them. Previous to the mills being started, they could get a comfortable competence, but year by year the margin of profit has been narrowed down, till at length absolute starvation is beginning to stare them in the face, and that within measurable distance.

To the above we may add again the various gipsy tribes, who have no settled homes or regular means of livelihood. Finally, there are the non-religious mendicants, the religious ones being considered as not coming within the scope of our present effort, being provided for in charitable institutions of their own.

Representatives of nearly all the above abound in our cities, and when both town and village destitutes come to be reckoned together, I do not think it will be too serious a view to take of their numbers, to reckon the absolutely workless as numbering at least 25 or 26 millions.

CHAPTER VII.
THE HOMELESS POOR.

On this question I do not propose to say much, not because there is not much that could be said, but because in a climate like India it is a matter of secondary importance as compared with food. The people themselves are comparatively speaking indifferent to it. The "bitter cry" of India if put into words would consist simply of "Give us food to fill our stomachs. This is all we ask. As for shelter, we are content with any hovel, or willing to betake ourselves to the open air. But food we cannot do without."

And yet, looked at from the point of view either of a moralist, a sanitarian, or a humanitarian, the question is one which calls for prompt consideration and remedial action. For instance, according to the last Government census, the average number of persons inhabiting each house in the city of Bombay is no less than 28. The average for the entire Presidency is six. But then it must be remembered that the great majority of the houses of the poor in the agricultural district consist of one-roomed huts, in which the whole family sleep together.

In the cities the overcrowding has become so excessive, and the accomodation available for the poor is so inadequate, costly and squalid, as to almost beggar description. Considerations of decency, comfort and health are largely thrown to the winds. A single unfurnished room, merely divided from the next one by a thin boarding, through which everything can be heard, will command from five to thirty rupees a month, and even more, according to its position, in Bombay.

The typical poor man's home in India consists as a rule of a single-storeyed hut with walls of mud or wattle, and roof of grass, palm-leaf, tiles, mud, or stones, according to the nature of the country. One or two rooms, and a small verandah, are all that he requires for himself and his family.

In the cities the high price of the land makes even this little impossible. Take for instance Bombay. Here the representative of the London lodging-house is to be found in the form of what are called "chawls," large buildings, several storeys high, divided up into small rooms, which are let off to families, at a rental of from three rupees a month and upwards. Very commonly the same room serves for living, sleeping, cooking, and eating. There being as a rule no cooking place, the cheap earthen "choola" serves as a sufficient make-shift, and the smoke finds its exit through the door or window best it can.

For hundreds, probably thousands, in every large city, even this poor semblance of a home does not exist. Those who manage somehow or other to live on nothing a month, cannot certainly afford to pay three rupees, or even less, for a lodging. Whilst, no doubt, many of the submerged, tenth are not absolutely houseless, inasmuch as they are often able to share the shelter of some relation or friend, it cannot be doubted that a very large percentage of them might say, "Foxes have holes, and the birds of the air have nests," but we "have not where to lay our heads."

Of the homeless poor there are two classes. The more fortunate find shelter in those of the Dharamsalas, Temples and Mosques which contain provision for such purposes. It must be remembered, however, that a large number of such institutions are reserved for certain favored castes, and are not therefore available for the out-caste poor. For the rest, the uncertain shelter of verandahs, porticoes, market-places, open sheds, and, in fine weather, the road-way, esplanade, or some shady tree, have to suffice.

As already said, I am quite willing to admit that this question of shelter for the poor is of secondary importance as compared with that of their food-supply. And yet is it nothing to us that millions of the Indian poor have no place that they can call "home," not even the meagre shelter of the one-roomed hut with which they would gladly be content? Is it nothing to us that superadded to the sufferings of hunger, they have to face the sharp and sometimes frosty air of the cold weather with scarcely a rag to their backs, and no doors, windows, or even walls to keep off the chilly wind? Is it nothing to us that in the rainy season they have to make their bed on the damp floor or ground, though to do so means a certain attack of fever? Is it nothing to us that under such circumstances the houseless poor should be converted into a dismal quagmire in which moral leprosy, more terrible than its bodily representative, should thrive and propagate itself? Certainly if the Indian destitute are to have a "bullock charter" granted to them, it will be necessary that it should sooner or later include suitable and decent shelter as well as food.

True, the problem is a vast one but this is no reason why it should be looked upon as insoluble, or left to grow year by year still vaster and more uncontrollable.

What we propose ourselves to undertake in this will be found elsewhere (see Part II Chapter VI). It must be remembered, moreover, that if our efforts to deal with the workless masses in finding them employment should prove successful this will in itself help to remove much of the existing evil. And by directing labor into channels where it can be the most profitably employed, we shall help to disembarrass those channels which have at present got choked up with an excess of it.

CHAPTER VIII.
THE LAND OF DEBT.

One of the darkest shadows on the Indian horizon is that of debt. A drowning man will snatch at a straw, and it would surely be inhuman for us to find much fault with the unhappy creatures who constitute the submerged tenth for borrowing their pittance at even the most exorbitant rates of interest in the effort to keep their heads above water.

I have no desire here to draw a gloomy picture of the Indian Shylock. In some respects I believe him to be a decided improvement on his European and Jewish representative. It was only a short time ago that I read a blood-curdling description of the London money-lender, which put any Indian I have ever come across altogether into the shade.

Nevertheless, Shylock flourishes in India as perhaps in no other country under the sun. His name is Legion. He is ubiquitous. He has the usual abnormal appetite of his fraternity for rupees. But strange to say he fattens upon poverty and grows rich upon the destitute. Whereas in other regions he usually concentrates his attention upon the rich and well-to-do classes, here he specially marks out for his prey those who if not absolutely destitute live upon the border-land of that desolate desert, and makes up by their numbers for what they may lack in quality. He gives loans for the smallest amount from a rupee and upwards, charging at the rate of half an anna per month interest for each rupee, which amounts to nearly 38 per cent. per annum. As for payment, he is willing to wait. Every three years, a fresh bond is drawn up including principal and interest. Finally, when the amount has been sufficiently run up, whatever land, house, buffalo, or other petty possessions may belong to the debtor are sold up, usually far below their real value.

I remember one case, which came before me when I was in Government service, where the facts were practically undisputed, in which a cultivator was sued for 900 rupees, principal and interest, the original debt being only ten rupees worth of grain borrowed a few years previously. Ultimately it was compromised for about 100 rupees. This is by no means an exceptional case.

Of course it may be said in favour of the money-lender that he is obliged to charge these high rates, to cover the extra risk, and that as a rule, he is generally prepared to forego half his legal claim when the time for payment comes. I am aware also that the subject has long occupied the earnest attention of Government, and that in some parts of the country enactments have been introduced for the relief of poor debtors. But these are only local and the evil is universal. A judicial Solon is sadly needed who shall rise up and boldly face the evil. The extortions of usurers have led to revolutions before now, and it seems high time for an enlightened Government to do something on a large scale for the abatement of the evil, if only by an absolute refusal to enforce any such usurious contracts.

But I have only mentioned the subject, because it plays a specially important part in the present depressed condition of the submerged masses. In the following pages I hope among other things to be able to cast some rays of light into this valley of the shadow of debt, if not of death.

CHAPTER IX.
THE LAND OF FAMINE.

Any review of Darkest India would be incomplete without some mention of the widespread and calamitous famines which periodically devastate the country and which reappear from time to time with terrible certainty.

In a country where so large a proportion of the population is agricultural, and where the poor are almost entirely paid in kind, the failure of a single crop means the most terrible scarcity and privation for those who even in time of plenty live at best but a hand-to-mouth existence. And when the failure is repeated famine faces the poverty-stricken masses, and they are frequently swept off by thousands.

In the terrible Madras famine of 1877 to 1878, several millions perished, in spite of the relief works and charitable agencies which hastened to their assistance. When the census of 1881 came to be taken, it was found that in this part of India, instead of the population having largely increased, as was everywhere else the case, there had been a diminution of two per cent as compared with the census of 1871.

It may be said that such famines are not frequent and we are thankful to admit that this is so. Yet scarcely a year passes without some part of India suffering severely from partial droughts. Only last year hundreds of poor starving wretches, crowded into Bombay from Kattiyawar, and were for weeks encamped on the Esplanade, an abject multitude, dependent on the charity of the rich. And yet it was "no famine" that had driven them hundreds of miles from their homes, but "only a scarcity."

At the same time famine prevailed in the Ganjam District to an extent which would probably have been utterly discredited, had not the Governor of Madras proceeded personally to the spot, and reported on the terrible state of affairs. No less than 30,000 persons were thrown upon Government for their support. In the same year through a fortnight's delay in the break of the monsoon, there were grain riots at Trichinopoly and Tanjore, several merchants stores being broken into, through a rise in the price of food. Happily a subsequent fall of rain averted the impending calamity, prices fell and order was restored.

Now to deal radically with famines it is necessary to meet them half way, and not to wait till they are upon us in all their stupendous immensity. It must be remembered that, as in the above instances, the present condition of things is such, that the mere threatening of famine is sufficient to send up the prices of food at a bound, to famine rates.

The chief victims of famine are the very classes who have been here described as constituting the "submerged tenth." In ordinary times "the wolf" is always "at the door" but at these calamitous periods there is no door to keep him out, and he is master of the situation. Now General Booth's scheme proposes to deal with him promptly and remove him to such a safe distance, as shall make his inroads almost impossible.

By leaving these destitute classes in their present miserable condition, we prepare for ourselves a gigantic and impossible task when the evil day of famine at last overtakes us. By facing the difficulty at the outset, and meeting it midway, we make our task much easier. Time is in our favour. True, the people are hungry, but they are not dying. We can afford to let them drift a few weeks, months, or even years longer, while we are putting our heads and hearts together to devise for them some way of deliverance commensurate with the immensity of their needs. But to resign oneself to the present condition of things as inevitable seems to me almost as heartless as to fold our hands helplessly at a time of absolute famine. To deafen our ears to the immediate distresses of the submerged tenth may be less criminal in degree but not in kind.

To those who feel paralysed by the vastness of the problem I would say "Study General Booth's Way Out and the adaptation of it to India which I have endeavoured to sketch in the following pages."

Here at least is a plan, perhaps not a perfect one, but still definite, tangible and immediately possible. Improve upon it as much as you like. Help us to remedy its defects by all means. But whatever you do, don't stand by as an indifferent spectator. Put your own individual shoulder to the wheel. Help us with your sympathy, prayers and substance to make the effort, and should failure ensue, you will at least have the satisfaction of realising that you have helped others to make an honest determined effort for dealing with a gigantic evil that involves the welfare, if not the existence of millions.

CHAPTER X.
THE LAND OF PESTILENCES.

Happily a description of English destitution does not call for any reference to plagues, such as those which annually or at least periodically, devastate India, and that with such certainty that their presence has come to be regarded, almost with indifference, as a matter of course, or at least of necessity. Indeed we suppose that some would even look upon it as a Divinely ordained method for reducing the population. True, that in Europe the matter is regarded in a very different light. Public opinion has made its voice heard. Medical science has exerted itself, and not in vain. The laws of sanitation are better known, and are enforced upon the entire community by severe legal enactments. And above all, Christianity has taught the rich to say of the poor "He is my brother," and to provide for him the medical care and attention that would otherwise not be within his reach.

What is possible in Europe is no doubt possible in India. Much has already been done, and our Government is fully awake to the importance of the subject, and will be able, year by year, to institute further improvements in this respect.

With this, however, we are not directly concerned. My object in referring to the subject is to point out--

1. That it is almost invariably from among the submerged tenth, with whom we propose to deal that these fearful plagues usually have their origin. Pestilence may indeed be said to take up its abode among them. Destitution is as it were the egg from which pestilence is hatched. There are brooding seasons when it may for a time disappear from sight. But it is there all the same and we know it. If we are to eradicate the evil, we must deal effectually with its cause. And this is the special object of General Booth's scheme.

True, it may be possible to keep this deadly enemy at bay by multiplying our hospital fortresses and putting into the field medical legions armed with the latest discoveries of science. But the requisite paraphernalia is too expensive for a country like India; and who does not know that well-fed bodies, and healthy homes are better safeguards against disease than all the most costly medicines that could be provided by the British pharmacopoeia? If therefore we are able to deal radically with destitution we shall at the same time strike an effective blow at the pestilences which are at present such a scourge to India.

2. Again I would like to remind my readers of another fact, and in this aspect of the question, all classes of the community are bound to be interested. If pestilence begins its deadly work among the destitute, it can never be reckoned on to stop there. Indeed pestilence may be regarded as *Nature's revenge* on society for the neglect of the poor. Once the cholera fiend has broken loose, it is impossible to tell whom he is going to select for his victims. The rich, the fair, the learned, the young, the strong, are often the first objects of his attention. He manifests a reckless disregard of social position. The distinctions of caste and rank, of beauty or learning, are not for him. And even as I write he may be preparing his invisible hordes of bacilli for fresh invasions, more terrible than those that have ever swept down from the mountains of Afghanistan. While we are spending millions upon strengthening our North-Western Frontiers against a foe who may never exist, save in our imagination, can we dare to neglect the more terrible enemy who defies all Boundary Commissions, who overleaps the strongest fortresses, and who laughs to scorn the largest cannon that ever capped our walls?

3. Finally there is one very sad shade in this part of our picture of darkest India. If on the one hand pestilence may be said to somewhat thin the ranks of the destitute by decreasing the number of mouths requiring to be fed, it must be remembered on the other hand that it continually recruits them both by sweeping away so many of the breadwinners, and by frequently paralysing many of those who are left, and preventing them from earning what they otherwise might. How often do we hear of even public institutions having to be closed, and of thousands being thrown out of work by the panic which ensues at such times.

I have sought to confine myself to a matter-of-fact description of this gloomy subject, and to avoid anything that could be construed into mere sensationalism.

And yet deaf must be the ears, and hard must be the hearts, that can be insensible to the cries of agony that yearly ascend from thousands and tens of thousands of homes. In a recent Government report, I find that from cholera alone in one year there were reported no less than 300,000 deaths; and yet the year was not remarkable for any exceptional outbreak. Still more terrible and regular are the ravages of the various malarial fevers, that sweep away millions yearly to a premature grave, often just in the prime of life, when they are most needed by the country. That a very large percentage of these deaths are directly connected with destitution, and that pestilence frequently but finishes the work commenced by months and years of starvation, is too notorious to require proof. It is a melancholy picture, and yet without it our review of Darkest India would be necessarily incomplete.

CHAPTER XI.
THE WHITE ANTS OF INDIAN SOCIETY.

Hitherto our description of the Submerged Tenth has concerned those who may be styled principally the children of misfortune, and who in their struggle for existence have resort to means which are indeed desperate in their nature, but against which no moral objection can be raised.

General Booth next calls attention to another great section of the Submerged Tenth who have found a temporary shelter or asylum in the temple of Vice,--those who either trade upon the sins of society, or are the miserable victims of those sins. The unlawful gratification of the natural appetites has ever been the snare by which millions have been deluded to damnation. If it were possible to combat this tendency in human nature by mere legal enactments, it would have been done long ago. But though much has been done in this way to hold vice in check, and to prevent it from openly parading itself in public as it otherwise would, yet it has chiefly been by the chains of religion that the monster has been bound, and even his legal shackles have mostly been manufactured at the anvils of the religious public. Take for instance the wholesale prohibition of intoxicating liquor by the Mahommedan religion, or again the strong Temperance movement that has more lately been established among Christians. The former has no doubt accomplished what would never have been done by means of legal enactments, while the latter has first educated the public on the Temperance question and has thus prepared the way for prohibitory legislation of a more stringent character.

In dealing with this portion of the Submerged Tenth there can be no doubt that the religious and moral appeals of the Salvation Army Officers will serve to stimulate and enforce wholesale reformation. By substituting the attractions of our public meetings, we shall do much to counteract those of the liquor den and other factories of pollution and destitution,--for it is as such that we may regard the places where drunkards, opium-eaters, prostitutes, fornicators, and the other hideous satellites of Vice are manufactured wholesale, whether with or without the shelter of a license. A large proportion of those who are engaged in vice as a trade openly profess to do so as a means of subsistence, and because it enables them to eke out what is in nine cases out of ten but a scanty subsistence, and what is almost invariably accompanied by the most terrible penalties Nature can inflict on those who outrage her ordinances. Many are heartily sick of the trade, but can see no way of escape. In dealing with destitution we shall open for these a door of hope. The deserters from the ranks of those who trade in vice will help us to deal more effectively with those who still cling to the profession on account of its profits.

In dealing with the panderers to the vices of society we shall largely diminish the numbers of its victims. It has been said that sinning is very much a matter of temptation, and in reducing those temptations, as we believe General Booth's scheme will largely tend to do, we shall be able to reduce in quantity, if we cannot hope to cause altogether to cease, the frightful holocaust of human victims that is annually offered up at this dark shrine.

(a) The Drunkards.

I will take the question of the Drunkard first, for it is itself a prolific root of all kinds of evil. The gradual breaking up of religious restraints, the increasing facilities for obtaining at smallest cost the most fiery and dangerous liquors, the added suffering entailed on any drinking habits that may be formed by the tropical heat of India, all serve to accentuate the gravity of the evil in this country. Add to this a consideration of the distressing poverty, the chronic hunger, the dull monotony, unrelieved by hope of amendment, in which myriads of the people of India fight out the battle of life; reflect how these must crave for the boon of forgetfulness and eagerly grasp at the wretched relief which drunkenness may bring. Nor can we throw the responsibility altogether upon the individual, if it be true that prior to contact with Western nations, the Hindoos were largely a temperate and even an abstinent people. We are in an especial manner bound to consider whether there can be found any alleviation or remedy for a disaster which, if we have not actually created, we have at least suffered to spring up unheeded and unchecked in our very midst.

It is notorious that the large cities of India are crowded with shops of the kind thus described by Mr. Caine, late M.P., in his "Picturesque India":

"The wide and spacious shops in front of which are strewn broken potsherds, and whose contents are two or three kegs and a pile of little pots; are the liquor-dealer's establishments. The groups of noisy men seated on the floor are drinking ardent spirits of the worst description absolutely forbidden to the British soldiers, but sold retail to natives at three farthings a gill."

Mr. Caine goes on to say that in the city of Lucknow, with a population of some 300,000 inhabitants, there were in 1889 thirty distilleries of native spirits and 200 liquor-shops. The Government exchequer receipts from spirits in the North-West Provinces amount to nearly L600,000, having doubled themselves during the last seven years. This means that in round numbers L1,000,000 worth of native spirits is sold in these provinces per annum.

Now consider first that as a rule with rare exceptions a native of India who uses the fiery country liquors drinks for no other purpose than to become intoxicated. They are manufactured with a view to this, and not as in Europe to provide a thirst-quenching potation. Mr. Caine says: "The people of India, unlike other people, only drink for the purpose of getting drunk, and if we make them drunken we destroy them more rapidly than by war, pestilence and famine."

Nothing is clearer than that a rapidly increasing multitude in this country, once remarkable for its sobriety and thrift, are rushing headlong into the disastrous vice of intemperance and its attendant horrors, almost without check. Something must be done. We cannot cold-bloodedly abandon them to a gospel of despair.

(b) The Opium Slaves.

Darker still perhaps is the dreadful night, and more sickening the miasma, which lies around the opium creeks, multiplying and increasing and slowly sucking down into their slimy depths thousands upon thousands of those who dare to seek momentary relief from sorrow in its lethal stream. Mr. Caine thus describes an opium den in Lucknow:--

"Enter one of the side rooms. It has no windows and is very dark, but in the centre is a small charcoal fire whose lurid glow lights up the faces of nine or ten human beings, men and women, lying on the floor. A young girl some fifteen years of age has charge of each room, fans the fire, lights the opium pipe, and holds it in the mouth of the last comer, till the head falls heavily on the body of his or her predecessor. In no East-end gin palace, in no lunatic or idiot asylum, will you see such horrible destruction of God's image in the face of man, as appears in the countenances of those in the preliminary stage of opium drunkenness! Here you, may see some handsome young married woman, nineteen or twenty years of age, sprawling, on the ground, her fine brown eyes flattened and dull with coming, stupor; and her lips drawn convulsively back from her glittering white teeth. Here is a young girl sitting among a group of newly arrived customers singing some romance. As they hand round the pipes there is a bonny little lad of six or seven watching his father's changing face with a dreadful indifference.

"At night these dens are crowded to excess, and it is estimated that there are upwards of twelve thousand persons in Lucknow enslaved by this hideous vice. An opium sot is the most hopeless of all drunkards. Once in the clutches of the fiend, everything gives way to his fierce promptings. His victims only work to get more money for opium. Wife, children, home, health, and life itself are sacrificed to this degrading passion."

If twelve thousand for Lucknow be a fair estimate, can we put the figures for the whole country at less than 100,000?

Still there is a deeper depth. In the same city, says Mr. Caine, there are ninety shops for the sale of Bhang and Churras. "Bhang," says the same writer, "is the most horrible intoxicant the world has ever produced. In Egypt its importation and sale is absolutely forbidden, and a costly preventive service is maintained to suppress the smuggling of it by Greek adventurers. When an Indian wants to commit some horrible crime such as murder, he prepares himself for it with two annas' worth of Bhang."

(c) Prostitution.

In the all but impenetrable shades and death-breathing swamps of this social forest, lie and suffer and rot probably not less than one hundred thousand prostitutes. Multitudes of these are dedicated to such a life in childhood, given over to it, in some cases by their parents and not unfrequently kept in connection with the temples. Thousands are searched for and persuaded and entrapped by old women, whose main business it is to supply the market. We know of at least one village where beautiful children, who have been decoyed or purchased from their parents by these prostitute-hunters, are taken to be reared and trained for the profession. In Bombay there is actually a caste in which the girls are in early childhood "married to the dagger," or, in other words, dedicated to a life of prostitution. In some of the cities old men are employed as touts to secure customers for the women, who remain in their haunts, thus seducing and leading into vice crowds of lads and young men who might otherwise have escaped.

Such suffering, shame, cruelty, and wreckage belong to this crime that one's heart bleeds to think of the tens of thousands doomed, not by their own choice, but by the wicked greed of unnatural parents or the crafty cunning of wicked decoys to such a gehenna, without the least power to extricate themselves from its torment and its shame.

With so much pity left upon the earth to weep over human woes, with so much courage still to hack and hew a path through grim forests and morasses of suffering, there must, and shall, be found "a way out."

CHAPTER XII.
THE CRIMINALS.

The most recent report of the Indian Government informs us that there are now no less that 737 Jails in British India (exclusive of Native Territory), with an average population of 75,922 prisoners. In the course of last year in the Bombay Presidency alone no less than 76,000 criminals were convicted, while 152,879 were placed on trial before the various courts. In the whole of India the number of annual convictions amount to upwards of one million, while the number who appear before the Court are at least twice as numerous. Again, there are also immense numbers of offences committed yearly, in which the Police are unable to get any clue, the offenders having succeeded in eluding altogether the vigilance of the Law. For instance a celebrated outlaw has only recently been apprehended in Central India after several years of successful and daring robbery, arson, mutilation and murder. Indeed in many parts of India there are predatory tribes and communities of thieves who have to be perpetually under Police surveillance, and who are brought up from their infancy to thieving as a profession.

We desire to plead the cause of the voiceless multitude who occupy our Indian Jails. The fact that they are voiceless,--that they have no means of voicing their claims, their wrongs and their rights (for they, too, *have* rights), only adds to their danger. How can a criminal hope for redress? What chance has he of being heard? Who will listen? What advocate will plead his cause? Ah, if he happen to be rich, it is true, he will have many friends! But as a rule the criminal is poor. Often he has to choose between crime and starvation. For himself he might prefer to starve, but the sight of his emaciated wife and aged parents,--with whom, criminal though he be, he is as a rule ready to share his last crust,--the clamour of his hungry children, all this drives him to desperation and to a life of crime. He can only give voice to his sorrows and his needs by some fresh act of lawlessness. Hence the occasional outbursts of mutiny, and the murders of jail warders, which from time to time reach the newspapers and shock the public ear.

And here I would desire to call attention to the fact that though crime must be vigorously dealt with and punished, at the same time the tendency of punishment is not to *reform*, but to *harden.* Who does not know that the *worst criminals* are those who have been *longest in Jail*? Instead of *getting better* they *grow daily worse*,--more adept in committing crime and eluding detection,--more careless as to its consequences.

Equally futile would be the offer of a wholesale pardon. A singular illustration of this occurred in 1887, when in honour of Her Majesty's Jubilee in the Bombay Presidency alone, no less than 2,465 prisoners were released out of a total of 6,087. Yet the Government report goes on to show that within a few months of their release the Jails were fuller than ever!

What, then, is to be done? Punishment hardens the criminal, pardon encourages crime, while the hearts of the offenders remain the same!

Here steps in the Salvation Army. Its methods and meetings, however distasteful to the educated and refined, have a special attraction for these dangerous classes. Its Officers are accustomed to handle them with superhuman love and patience, as well as with a tact and adroitness such as has often elicited the admiration and praise of those who have no sympathy with our creed or ways of work.

We have all over the world fearlessly invaded these criminals in their lowest haunts and dens, in the teeth of the warnings of the Police; we have braved their fiercest fury when, urged on by publicans, maddened with drink, misled by all sorts of infamous lies, and winked at or patronised by the Police and Magistrates, they have wreaked on us the utmost cruelties. We have invariably weathered the storm, though often at the cost of health and even life itself. And in the end as a rule the Roughs, Criminals and Dangerous Classes have become our warmest friends and vigorous supporters. From amidst them we have rescued and reformed some of the noblest trophies of Divine grace. This has been done all over the world. It has been done in India and Ceylon. In a later part of this book we have given a glimpse of this most interesting and important portion of our work. Independent witnesses testify to its reality. Government officials assure us of their warmest sympathy, and in not a few cases aid us with their influence and subscriptions. In Ceylon the Government has treated us most handsomely, throwing open their prisons for our Officers to visit and hold meetings among the prisoners, assisting us in the expenses of our Home with a monthly grant of Rs. 100, and encouraging the criminal classes to take advantage of the opportunity thus afforded them for reforming their lives.

The common reason given for refusing such assistance elsewhere is that Government cannot interfere with the religion of the prisoners. But in Ceylon the majority of the prisoners are Buddhists, Hindoos and Mahommedans, and what has been found to work so well there can surely be tried with equal success elsewhere! Government does not hesitate all over India to assist religious bodies in their endeavours to *educate* the people, and they may therefore well countenance and help forward, as they might so easily do, our efforts to reach and reform the criminal classes on precisely the same grounds, offering similar advantages to any Hindoo or Mahommedan Associations that might afterwards be formed for the same purpose. At present the Indian criminal has no friend to lend him a helping hand. Prison officials in various places have personally informed me that they are distressed at being able to do nothing for criminals, who, having lost their character and being abandoned by their friends, have no alternative but to return to their old associates. If our example causes others to rise up and make efforts for reaching and reforming these classes, who would not rejoice? At present it is a sad fact that throughout India the native criminals are debarred from all opportunities of being reached by the softening influences of religion. The Europeans have their Chaplains,--the Natives are allowed to have no one to minister to their souls' needs, or to bring to bear upon them those moral influences which might, and we know often would, lead to their reform. There seems no reason whatever why the following rules, which have been drawn up by the Ceylon Government, should not be adopted likewise in India:--

General Rules made by His Excellency the Governor, acting under the advice of the Executive Council for the Government of Prisons, for the guidance of the prison officers, under and by authority of Section 26 *of the Prisons Ordinance*, 1887.

226. Ministers of religion and religions instructors shall be

entitled to visit prisoners under commitment for trial and prisoners undergoing sentence after trial, and to give religious and moral instructions to those who are willing to receive the same on Sundays and other days in which prisoners are usually allowed freedom from work, between the hours of eight in the morning and four in the afternoon.

227. Such ministers or other persons shall be allowed access at all times (but between the hours specified) to all prisoners who shall be certified by the medical officers of the prison to be seriously ill.

228. In prisons where such an arrangement can conveniently be made, a suitable room shall be set apart where religious instruction can be afforded to prisoners and the rites of religion administered.

229. If, under the directions of Government, Christian services be held in any Jail, on Sundays and on other days when such services are performed, all Christian criminal prisoners shall attend the same unless prevented by sickness or other reasonable cause--to be allowed by the Jailor--or unless their service is dispensed with by the Superintendent. No prisoner, however, shall be compelled to attend any religious instruction given by the ministers or religious instructor of a church or persuasion to which the prisoner does not belong.

230. It shall be lawful for the Superintendent in charge of any prison to prohibit any particular minister or instructor visiting any prisoner in such prison, if it shall appear to him that such minister or instructor is an improper or indiscreet person, or likely to have improper communication with the prisoner, provided that such Superintendent shall without delay communicate his reason for doing so, to the Inspector General for report to Government.

231. No books or printed papers shall be admitted into any prison for the use of the prisoners, except by permission of the Superintendent, and the jailor shall keep a catalogue of all books and printed papers admitted into the prison.

232. It shall be the duty of the minister or instructor admitted to visit any prison, to communicate to the jailor any abuse or impropriety in the prison which may come to his knowledge, on pain of being prohibited from visiting the prison.

CHAPTER XIII.
ON THE BORDER LAND.

Besides the 25,000,000 who constitute the actual destitute and criminal population, we estimate that at a very low computation there are 25,000,000 who are on the border-land, who are scarcely ever in a position to properly obtain for themselves and for their families the barest necessities of existence. I do not say that they are wholly submerged, but they pass a sort of amphibious existence, being part of the time under water and part of the time on land,--some part of their life being spent in the most abject poverty, and some part of it in absolute starvation--positively for the time submerged, and liable at any moment to be lastingly engulfed. These are the classes whose income never rises above five rupees a month, while more frequently it is under four rupees.

On one farm, concerning which we have detailed information, where the rent of the land is unusually low, the soil good and well irrigated, where loans can be got at a merely nominal interest, the cultivators, with the additional help of occasional cooly work, did not average in their earnings four rupees a month, some having to keep a family on three and a half, while if a bullock died, or a plough had to be procured, it meant positive hunger and increased indebtedness to supply those needs.

The fact is that in many districts there is not only an increase of population to be sustained by a constantly narrowing area of cultivated land, but the land itself is deteriorating through the unendurable pressure put upon it. As the forests grow more distant through being used up for timber and fuel, wood becomes dearer. The manure which ought to go upon the land is therefore by necessity consumed for fuel. The ground in consequence becomes impoverished. As the struggle for existence becomes fiercer, the people are unable to let their land periodically lie fallow, so the crops grow lighter. Again, the ryot is not only unable properly to feed himself, but his bullocks share a similar fate. The feeble animals can only draw a plough which merely scratches the surface of the ground. Furthermore, as the population increases the land is divided into smaller and smaller holdings. The struggle against the advancing tide of adversity cannot be maintained. Inch by inch the tide rolls up, pushing the border-landers closer and closer upon the black rocks of famine, to escape which they at length plunge into the sea amongst the submerged millions, who, weary and bitter and despairing, or with blind submission to the iron hand of fate, have grown hopelessly and miserably indifferent.

Now, it is notorious that millions live thus on the border-land. Granted that after the harvest border-landers may for a time get two good meals a day. Yet as the reserve store dwindles down and long before harvest-time comes round, again, they get but one, and that frequently a scanty one. They do live, multitudes of them, it is true, amidst conditions that seem to us impossible. But how many of them die on this one meal a day, there is nobody to chronicle. But if we do nothing beyond rescuing a considerable mass of the totally submerged, we shall considerably ameliorate the condition of these border-landers.

By rendering independent of charity thousands who now depend upon the gifts of the more fortunate, by making large tracts of land productive which at present lie waste, by enlarging the stream of emigration, and partially draining the morass of crime, it is absolutely certain that the conditions of life will become more favourable for the border-landers. New markets will be created both for produce and labour, which will tend to relieve the congested condition of the land now under cultivation.

The land at present is like a good, but overworked and under-fed horse, which, under this double adversity of overwork and under-feeding, dies and leaves his poor owner, who was entirely dependent upon his earnings, a pauper. It is a condition of things which is bad, and bound of necessity to grow only worse and worse, till the willing horse drops under his load, and his master falls from poverty to destitution. Once enable the man to temporarily decrease his horse's labour and permanently increase its food supply, that horse will regain its strength, and by its increased strength become able to do double the amount of work, increase its master's earnings, and so in time enable him not only to properly feed his horse, but also to properly feed himself.

Now close to hand there is an unemployed horse available which will afford the relief, for want of which the overworked horse is dying. The unoccupied and waste lands, waste labour, and waste produce, constitute the ideal unemployed horse, on whose back we would put part of the burden of maintaining the life and feeding the mouths of the Nation. This idle and hitherto useless horse will immediately become useful and productive, and will enable its under-fed companion, not only to be relieved of part of its burden, but also to get sufficient food, and grow once more plump and strong. Thus the man, or nation, that lived, however miserably, yet still lived, on the labour of the one famished over-worked horse, will then be able to get a decent living, since there will be two strong well-fed horses to work for them, instead of a single broken-down one.

It is simply impossible within the limits of this chapter to trace out the whole process. Enough to say that as a rule, to which of course there are exceptions, one man's prosperity means some one else's prosperity. Suppose I am a beggar. I wear practically no clothing. The little I have is what somebody else has cast off. I have no home. I sleep in the street. I get very little food, and that I do not pay for. I produce nothing. My children, if I have any, are wastrels like myself. But I am lifted out of this beggary, I become a productive worker. I get a home, wear clothes, buy food, educate my children. Not only have I improved my own circumstances, but I have helped to improve the circumstances of others. Builders, shopkeepers, food-producers, all profit by my redemption.

Now, if not one wastrel only, but 1,000,000 such are raised, a mighty impetus is given to industry of every kind, and the border-landers, instead of being driven on the black rocks by the tide of adverse surroundings, begin to drive back the tide, and conquer the earth, and subdue it, till the border-landers will be border-landers no longer, and the dreadful days of hunger will live only in the stories of famine and want, which the grey old man will tell to his happy and prosperous grandchildren, and ten thousand links of love between emigrant sons and home-staying fathers will bind the fertile plains of Ceylon, Burmah, Africa, and other countries to the populous shores of India.

CHAPTER XIV.
ELEMENTS OF HOPE.

The picture which I have endeavoured to paint in the foregoing pages is dark enough to strike despair into the hearts of the most sanguine. And if there were indeed no way of escape for these victims of sin and misfortune, we might well prefer to draw a veil over the sad scene, and to bury in the ocean of forgetfulness, the very recollection of this earthly purgatory.

But there are elements of hope in the consideration of this problem, which should prevent us from regarding it despair.

1. In the first place, supposing that we are correct in computing this human wastage at from twenty-five to twenty-six million souls, this would represent only some five million families. It is true that looked at even in this light the number is vast. But surely it is not impossible for India to make sufficient and suitable provision for them within her own borders, to say nothing of the "regions beyond" if reasonable thought and effort were put forth in dealing with the problem.

2. Again, as regards the **numbers**, it will be found **easier** to deal with these great national problems in bulk than piecemeal, and their very size will give them an impetus when once they are fairly set in motion. It will be found as easy to dispose of 1,000 people as of a hundred, and of 50,000 as of a thousand, if they be properly organised. Indeed, for many reasons it is easier. The larger the community, the more work they at once provide for each other. Once let this social ball be set rolling on a large scale, and we may believe that it will soon get to move of its own weight.

3. Again, it is not an indiscriminate system of largely extended charity that we propose to provide. Our object is to find work for these workless multitudes, and such work as shall more than pay for the very humble pittance the Indian destitute

requires. He must be a poor specimen of a human being who cannot fairly earn his anna or two annas a day, and our brains must be poor addled affairs, if in this great vast world of ours we cannot find that amount of work for him to do. It is all nonsense to talk about over-population, when the world is three parts empty and waiting to be occupied.

4. While we are piercing the bowels of the earth in search of gold, minerals and coal, there lies at our very door a mine of wealth which it is simple folly for us to ignore. True, the shaft has become choked with the rubbish of despair, vice and crime, which will take time, trouble and untiring patience to dig through. But it needs no prophet to foresee that beneath this rubbish are veins of golden ore which will amply repay our utmost efforts to open up. The old adage that "labour is wealth," and that a nation's riches consist in its hardy sons and daughters of toil, will yet be proved true. Treat this human muck-heap even as you would ordinary sewage or manure, and who does not know that the very same putrefying mass of corruption which if allowed to remain near our doors would breed nothing but fever, cholera, and the worst forms of disease and death, when removed to a little distance, will double and treble the ordinary fertility of the soil and produce crops that will increase the wealth of the entire nation?

And knowing this can we be so blind, even to our selfish interests, as to treat this human waste in a manner that we should deem the very height of imprudence and folly in dealing with the other sort? Can we shut our eyes to the fact that there are moral diseases, more terrible in their nature, and more fatal to a nation's life, than the bodily ones, against which we are so anxious to guard, even at the most lavish expenditure of the public purse? And shall we, in dealing with this moral sewage, neglect even the most ordinary precautions that we consider necessary in dealing with the conservancy of our cities?

If on the other hand the problem be boldly and wisely faced, I am convinced that in India, as in England, General Booth's most sanguine prophecies will be realised, our most pestilential marshes shall be drained, our moral atmosphere purified, prosperity take the place of destitution, and hope that of despair. The millstone that hangs around our national neck, so that we can barely keep our heads above water, even when there is not a ripple upon its surface, and that always threatens to engulf us in perdition at the first symptoms of a storm,--this millstone shall be converted into an unsinkable life-buoy, that shall not only support itself upon the crest of the highest waves, but shall help to keep afloat the entire national body. What is now an eyesore shall become an adornment, and what is now a cause of weakness shall be a source of strength, bulwark of protection and mine of wealth to all India. How this can be done we have sought in the following pages to unfold, adhering carefully to the programme marked out by General Booth, and suggesting only such additions and alterations as the circumstances of the case appear to necessitate.

PART II.--THE WAY OUT.

CHAPTER I.
THE ESSENTIALS TO SUCCESS.

General Booth prefaces his scheme for the deliverance of the submerged by laying down briefly the essentials to success. I cannot do better than quote from his own words.

(1) "You must *change the man*, when it is his character and conduct which constitute the reasons for his failure in the battle of life. No change in circumstances, no revolution in social conditions, can possibly transform the nature of man. Some of the worst men and women in the world, whose names are chronicled by history with a shudder of horror, were whose who had all the advantages that wealth, education and station could confer, or ambition could obtain.

"The supreme test of any scheme for benefiting humanity lies in the answer to the question; what does it make of the individual? Does it quicken his conscience, does it soften his heart, does it enlighten his mind? Does it, in short, make a true man of him? Because only by such influences can he be enabled to lead a human life. You may clothe the drunkard, fill his purse with gold, establish him in a well furnished house, and in three, six, or twelve months, he will once more be on the "Embankment," haunted by delirium tremens, dirty, squalid and ragged.

(2) "The remedy, to be effectual, must *change the circumstances*, when they are the cause of his wretched condition, and lie beyond his control.

(3) "Any remedy worthy of consideration must be on *a scale commensurate with the evil*, which it proposes to deal with. It is no use trying to bale out the ocean

with a pint pot. There must be no more philanthropic tinkering, as if this vast sea of human misery were contained in the limits of a garden pond.

(4) "Not only must the scheme be large enough, but it *must be permanent.* That is to say, it must not be merely spasmodic coping with the misery of to-day, but must go on dealing with the misery of to-morrow and the day after, so long as there is misery left in the world with which to grapple.

(5) "But while it must be permanent, it must also be *immediately practicable*, and capable of being brought into instant operation with beneficial results.

(6) "The indirect features of the scheme must not be such as to produce injury to the persons whom we seek to benefit. Mere charity for instance, while relieving the pinch of hunger, demoralises the recipient. It is no use conferring sixpenny worth of benefit on a man, if at the same time we do him a shillings worth of harm.

(7) "While assisting one class of the community, it must not seriously interfere with the interest of another.

"These are the conditions by which I ask you to test the scheme I am about to unfold. They are not of my making. They are the laws which govern the work of the philanthropic reformer just as the laws of gravitation, of wind and of weather govern the operation of the engineer. It is no use saying we could build a bridge across the Tay, if the wind did not blow. The engineer has to take into account the difficulties, and make them his starting point. The wind will blow, therefore the bridge must be made strong enough to resist it. So it is with the social difficulties, which confront us. If we act in harmony with these laws we shall triumph. But if we ignore them, they will overwhelm us with destruction, and cover us with disgrace."

CHAPTER II.
WHAT IS GENERAL BOOTH'S SCHEME?

H is object is to supply the destitute with food, shelter and clothing, to provide them with work and to set them on their feet for making a fresh start in life.

With a view to this he proposes to call into existence, a threefold organisation, consisting of self-helping and self-sustaining communities, governed and disciplined on the principles of the Salvation Army. These he calls "Colonies", and divides into

      (1) The City Colony,

      (2) The Country Colony, and

      (3) The Over-sea Colony.

All these are to be linked together and to be interwoven with and dependent on each other. In the City Colony a series of agencies will be established for gathering up and sifting the destitute. Thence they will be passed on to the Country Colony and subsequently many of them will be sent to Colonies across the sea.

Now this triple organisation can be brought into existence, on the largest possible scale in India under circumstances peculiarly favorable to the success of the scheme.

Our country is not of limited extent like England. It covers an immense area and includes a conglomeration of nationalities, such as we find in Europe, with the special advantage of being united under a single, and that a friendly Government.

Then again there is the fact that, though the influx from the country to the cities has commenced, yet it has not at present got beyond manageable proportions, so that it is possible for us, if awake to the emergency, to rise up and divert the stream into more desirable channels.

If instead of waiting for a further irruption of village Goths and Vandals, (which is only a matter of time, and which will soon overwhelm our City labour market and compel the attention of our civil authorities,) we anticipate the event and meet them half way by opening up fresh channels for them, more in harmony with their own taste and preference, we shall not only confer an inestimable boon upon them, but shall turn them into a source of strength and revenue for the country, and shall with them people tracts which are at present barren and fruitless, but which are only waiting to be occupied and which in many cases have only to be restored to the prosperity that they formerly enjoyed.

Finally we have the great advantage of a people already trained to husbandry from their youth, and accustomed to the very co-operative system of farming which General Booth advocates, where payments are mostly to be made in kind rather than in cash, and where the exchange of goods will largely supersede transactions in money, a strong but paternal government regulating all for the general good.

CHAPTER III.
THE CITY COLONY.

The first portion of General Booth's threefold scheme consists of the City Colony.

This may aptly be compared to a dredger, which, gathers up all the silt of a harbour, and carries it out to sea, leaves it there and then returns to repeat the operation. If such an operation is necessary in a harbour, and if without it the best anchorages in the world would often get choked with rubbish and become useless, how doubly important must it be in the case of the human wastage that abounds in every large Indian City.

Should a single ship strike on an unknown rock, we hasten to mark it down in our charts, or erect over the spot a lighthouse as a warning to others. Should it sink where it is likely to hinder the traffic, we set our engineers to work to remove it, even though it may be necessary to blow it to atoms.

And yet it is a notorious fact that our cities abound with rocks over which there is no lighthouse,--that every channel is obstructed with sunken vessels, and that there are not a few tribes of pirates who fatten on the human wreckage. But we fold our hands in despair, and allow bad to grow worse, till the problem daily becomes more enormous, desperate and difficult to deal with.

Now General Booth's scheme proposes to establish a dredger for every harbour, a lighthouse for every rock, an engineer for keeping clear every channel. It may be too much to expect that there will be no wrecks, but they will be fewer, and that surely is something! We do not say that there will be no accidents, but there will be willing hands held out to deliver. We cannot hope to abolish failures, mistakes, shortcomings and weaknesses of various sorts, but we shall do our best to anticipate and provide for them? We are sure there will be difficulties and disappointments to encounter, but we shall meet them in the confidence that God is on our side, that He is intensely interested in the efforts which He Himself has inspired us to undertake and that ultimate victory is bound to crown our efforts.

And now I would give a brief description of this great City Dredger, explaining its component parts in the chapters that are to follow. We cannot promise that the entire machine will get into working order at once. We are anxious to start it immediately and to complete it as soon as possible. But on the public will largely depend the question as to how long it will take us to get it afloat and finished. Its simplicity, practicability, and universality are to me at the same time its chief charms, and its credentials to success. It is only part of a larger scheme with which it is entwined. But it is an important, perhaps the most important part and will continue to exercise over the entire effort the controlling head and the inspiring heart without which the whole apparatus will be as motionless as a machine without steam, or a body without life.

The following are the various branches of the City Colony--

(1) The Regimentation of Labor.

(2) Food for all--Food Depots.

(3) Work for all--Labor yards.

(4) Shelter for all.

(5) The household Salvage Corps.

(6) The Prison Gate Brigade.

(7) The Drunkard's Home.

(8) The Rescue Home for fallen women.

(9) The poor man's Metropole.

(10) The Emigration Bureau.

To these no doubt will in course of time be added many other branches. In the meantime this is in itself a sufficiently extensive programme for some years to come. How we propose to elaborate each of the above, will be found in the following pages.

CHAPTER IV.
THE LABOR BUREAU.

One of the most painful sights with which modern civilisation presents us is the enormous and increasing wastage of valuable human labor. The first step towards remedying this gigantic and alarming evil will be to ascertain its extent. This we propose to do by means of our Labor Bureau. Here all classes of out-of-works will be welcomed, from the respectable well educated intelligent youths, who are being poured out of our colleges by thousands, to the most squalid specimen of a Lazarus that lies at our gates desiring to be fed with the crumbs that fall from our tables. All will be sorted out, sifted and regimented, or organised, into distinct corps, which will in time no doubt develope into legions.

The Bureau will not, however, stop short with simply ascertaining the extent of the evil which exists. It will at the same time turn its attention to the examination and regimentation of the channels which already exist for the absorption of that labor. For while it is true that there are vast quantities of unutilised labor, and that the present supply of labor greatly exceeds the demand, it is also true that for want of suitable arrangements for bringing together capital and labor, the capitalist also frequently loses time and money, either in searching for labor which he cannot get, or in resorting to labor of an inferior quality, where labor of a superior quality would bring in much larger returns.

Into the pre-existing channels it would be the first aim of our Labor Bureau to pour the labor supply of the country. And experience would probably enable us to widen, deepen and lengthen these channels in such a manner as would prove profitable to both employers and employed, as well as to the nation at large.

When, however, this had been done, it is alas! only too certain that we should still have left upon our hands a vast amount of surplus labor, for which we should next proceed to dig out new and profitable channels. The problem no doubt bristles with difficulties, but that is no reason why we should sit down before it and fold our hands in despair.

Once upon a time, aye for hundreds of years, the waters of the Cauvery were poured in one useless torrent into the sea, sweeping past great tracts of thirsty land, which craved its waters, but could not reach them. At the present moment scarcely a drop of that river reaches the ocean. Its course has been diverted into a thousand channels, and so fertilising are its waters that the rich alluvial deposits which they bear render the use of manure unnecessary. And yet for centuries these possibilities were unrecognised and suffered to go to waste.

Is not this a fitting picture of the huge river of labor that winds its course through arid plains of want and poverty and starvation, which it is capable of fertilising and converting into a modern Paradise? True that on its banks and in its immediate neighbourhood are strips of luxuriant vegetation. But those only show up in painful relief the utter barrenness of the "region beyond." Why should the dwellers upon the banks be allowed to monopolise and appropriate that which they cannot even utilise, and that which is often a source of positive danger, annoyance and loss to them? Why should not channels be devised for these human waters, by means of which they should be distributed, so as to be put to the utmost possible use?

This social problem is no doubt the "white elephant" of society. Cannot we devise a "kheddah" for capturing the entire herd wholesale? Perhaps after all we shall find it easier and quicker to catch and tame the herd, than to set snares and pitfalls for individual ones and twos. Ah, you say, many have tried and failed. That is because they have not studied the habits of the animal. Besides it is by means of failure that the grandest successes have ultimately been achieved. See how skilfully that "mahaut" manages his huge yet obedient servant. And cannot we point already in our own ranks to elephants more wonderful that have been tamed and mastered by the goad of love?

It is the successes of the past that encourage General Booth to face the problem in the spirit of hopefulness that breathes through every page of "Darkest England." And if the genius of man has been able to tame the strongest of animals, such as elephants,--the fiercest, such as lions,--the swiftest, such as horses, and the dullest, such as the ass,--why should we despair of reducing to order this chaotic mass of labor, and of turning that which at present constitutes a danger that threatens the very existence of society into a source of safety, of wealth and power? At any rate this is the object that will be kept steadily in view by our Labor Bureau.

All persons will be able to register names at our Bureau. If they are destitute and willing to go to our yards, they will be sent there and given work suitable to their caste, or profession. If on the other hand they are not in need of such assistance, being supported by their friends, we shall simply register their names and do our best to find suitable work for them, though it would of course be distinctly understood by them that we undertook no responsibility in regard to this. A small fee will be charged, in proportion to the nature of the case. This would serve to cover the expenses of the Bureau, which would I am sure meet a long felt want.

Employers of labour would benefit almost more even than the men employed, as we should always be able to supply them at a short notice with any description and number of "hands" that they might require, and they would be saved the expense, delay, and uncertainty of having to advertise.

For instance I know of millowners who complain that they cannot get labourers who will stay, and that their work suffers from the flotsam, jetsam character of those whom they employ working for a few weeks and then leaving. This we should be able to remedy.

Indeed after a short time we might reasonably expect that in recognising the great convenience thus afforded them, millowners and other great employers of labour, including very possibly the Government and the Railway Companies would refuse to employ any who had not registered themselves at our Bureau.

Again it would doubtless be a great satisfaction to employers in cases where a reduction of establishment became necessary, to feel that they could hand over to us those with whose services they were dispensing, knowing that every effort would be made to make suitable provision for them.

The labour register would contain columns in which would be entered the various kinds of employment for which the applicant was willing or suited, and the minimum pay which he was prepared to accept, so that we should be able to ascertain exactly how many out-of-works there were of each particular class. We should also enter in a separate register those who had accepted an inferior position, in the hopes of being able to better themselves subsequently.

In connection with our registers we should keep a character roll. Copies of certificates would be filed, and notes made in regard to unsatisfactory characters, so that in course of time we should be able to give some sort of a guarantee in regard to those whom we sent out. In the case of any one being reported to us as unsatisfactory, we should still, however, give him another chance by redrafting him into our Labour Yards, or by giving him some sort of inferior employment, more immediately under our own surveillance, till he had regained his character.

Among other things we might undertake to supply servants to European families. A register of such would be very useful both to masters and servants. For instance in the case of lost "chits" we could supply certified copies of the original.

There is another class to whom I should think the establishment of such an agency will be particularly welcome. Our cities swarm with educated young men unable to find employment. Although we cannot include them among our destitute classes, we believe that without turning aside from our main object, we could do a great deal to help them.

If our scheme grows to the proportions and with the rapidity which we anticipate, this would in itself absorb large numbers of them. And where we could do no more we could obtain a moral influence over them and they would come within the scope of the Advice and Intelligence Bureaux which are described elsewhere. Constituting as they do the cream of the youth of India, full of ardent, though often misdirected, enthusiasm, we should be able to help mould them into happy, independent, prosperous and loyal citizens, who would be a bulwark to the State, instead of leaving them to simmer in their present unfortunate circumstances. "To dig" they don't know, and "to beg" they are ashamed.

They would in their turn I believe give an important impetus to our scheme and might constitute themselves its fervent apostles helping it to sweep from end to end of India in less time than it is possible for us to conceive.

CHAPTER V.
FOOD FOR ALL--THE FOOD DEPOTS.

In England, owing to the severity and uncertainty of the weather, the food and shelter questions go hand in hand. This is not the case in India, where the shelter is not so important as the food, and there is no such urgency in dealing with the former as with the latter. For instance during nine months out of twelve it is not such a very great hardship to sleep in the open air in most parts of India. I have myself done it frequently and so have many of our Officers. It is true that we should not like it as a regular thing, and still less perhaps, if driven to it by absolute want. Still I am perfectly prepared to admit that the circumstances are totally different to that of England, and that the question of shelter is of secondary importance as compared with food.

The time will come when we shall be obliged to face and deal with it. If our scheme meets with the success that we anticipate, having first satisfied the gnawings of these hunger-bitten stomachs, we shall certainly turn round and think next what we can do to provide them with decent homes for themselves and their families.

But we can safely afford to defer the consideration of this question for the present, in order to throw all our time and energy into the solution of the infinitely more urgent and important problem of a regular and sufficient food supply for these destitutes.

At present as I have already pointed out, they are dependent solely on the help of relations and friends and on the doles of the charitable; or on the proceeds of vice and crime. The insufficiency of these to meet the needs of the case I have also, I believe, proved to demonstration.

Therefore one of the first parts of our City programme will be the establishment of cheap food depots, at which food of various kinds will be supplied at the lowest possible cost price. These depots will be dovetailed in with other parts of our scheme, which have yet to be described, and the one will help to support the other.

It may be objected that if we undertake to sell food at lower than the ordinary market rates, we shall interfere with the legitimate operations of trade. But to this we would answer that the same objection would be still more true in regard to charitable doles, which are given for nothing. And further, we shall fix our prices with a view to covering the actual cost of the food, so that there will not be any probability of our interfering with ordinary market rates. Besides, should there be any very serious difficulty of the kind, we could always make a rule limiting the food sold at these depots to those who came under the operation of the other branches of our social reform.

At the outset it would probably be wisest to avoid all caste complications by confining ourselves entirely to uncooked food, leaving the people to do their own cooking, but it is very probable that before long we should be forced to undertake the preparation of cooked food. We should of course pay due regard in this respect to the customs of the various castes, religions and nationalities concerned. To a Hindoo for instance it would be extremely disagreeable to eat out Of the same dish as others, while Mahommedans, as one said to me the other day, only enjoy the meal the more, when others are sitting round the platter. These, however, are subordinate details which would largely settle themselves as we went along. Food in some shape or form, the destitute must have, good in quality and sufficient in quantity, and if they prefer it uncooked this will save us trouble, whereas if cooking becomes necessary we shall have another industry for the employment of many hands. Meanwhile the fact that nearly every native of the poorer castes, be it man, woman, or even child, knows how to cook their own food, is likely to be of no little help in settling the question of the food supply.

CHAPTER VI.
WORK FOR ALL, OR THE LABOUR YARD.

But it may next be asked, what we shall do in the case of those who have no money with which to buy their food, even at the reduced rates we would propose? To this we would reply that such will be expected to perform a reasonable amount of work, in return for which they will be given tickets entitling them to obtain food from the depots just referred to.

In order to do this we shall establish labour yards, where we shall provide work of a suitable character for the destitute. This will involve very little expense, as sheds of a cheap description will answer our purpose, there being no necessity for providing against the inclement weather which adds so greatly to the expense and difficulty of carrying on such operations in England.

Whatever may be the produce of this cheap labour, we shall be careful to sell it rather above than below the ordinary market rates, so as to avoid competing with other labour. Moreover, we shall direct our attention from the first to manufacturing chiefly those articles which are likely to be of service to us in other branches of our scheme, so that the labour of the destitute will go chiefly towards supplying their own wants and those of the persons who are engaged in prosecuting the work.

For instance, supposing that a number of the destitute were employed in making coarse cloth, baskets, mats, or cow-dung fuel, these could be retailed at a nominal figure to those who presented our labour tickets at our food depots.

The most encouraging feature in the establishment of labour yards is that nearly every Indian has been brought up from childhood to some trade. You can rarely meet the most ignorant and uneducated Native without finding that he is thoroughly expert at some kind of handicraft. In brigading the poor we should be careful to make the best use of this knowledge by putting each as much as possible to the trade with which he was most familiar.

The following industries, the majority of them directly connected with various branches of our work, could be started at once and would need scarcely any outlay to begin with.

1. *The Potters Brigade*--Would furnish us with the earthenware, for which we should from the first have a very large demand. The Household Salvage Brigade would require some thousands of pots to start with and in connection with our food depots we should be able to dispose of thousands more.

2. *The Weavers Brigade*--This would give employment for a large number of skilled hands. Their first object would be to supply the kinds of clothes, blankets, &c., which would be most suitable for the use of the submerged tenth. In catering for their wants we should avoid, however, anything *prisony*, or *workhousey*, or charity-institutiony in appearance. As our numbers increased we should find plenty of work for our weavers, at any rate for many years to come without entering into any sort of competition either with the market or the mills.

3. *The Basket Brigade*--Would supply us with all sorts of cheap baskets, for which we should have a constant demand.

4. *The Mat Making Brigade*--Would find employment for many more hands in supplying us with mats for sleeping and household purposes.

5. *The Fuel Brigade*--Here we have an industry which requires no skill. There would be two branches of it--the woodchoppers and the Oopala makers. For the latter women and children could be largely employed both in the collection of the cow-dung and in the preparation of it for use as fuel.

6. *The Tinners Brigade*--Will be kept busy making receptables and badges for the Salvage Brigade, and also probably emblems for the Labor Bureau.

7. *The Ropemakers Brigade*--Will furnish employment to a number more and the results of their labour will find an ample market in our various colonies.

8. *The Tanners Brigade*--Will supply all our departments with such leather as may be required for various purposes, and among other things will be attached to.

9. *The Shoemakers Brigade*--Who will be employed in patching up the old shoes collected by our Household Salvage Brigade and in making new ones for our consumption.

10. *The Tailors Brigade*--Will supply uniform and clothing of all kinds. For these we have already a very considerable demand, which would increase year by year.

11. *The Carpenters Brigade*--Would have plenty to do in providing seats for our Barracks, office essentials, boxes, and household furniture for our colonies. They would be linked with

12. *The Building Brigade*--For whom we shall find ample employment in the erection of our Labour Sheds, Shelters and Farms.

13. *The Masons Brigade*--Would also be attached to the previous one, and would become an important feature in our Labour Department.

14. *The Brick Makers Brigade*--Would supply us with all the bricks and tiles that we might require. Here again it is easy to see that, without trenching in the least on the outside public, we should

create and support an important industry which would soon absorb hundreds if not thousands of hands.

15. *The Painters Brigade*--Would undertake the painting and whitewashing of our buildings, carts, tinware, &c.

16. *The Dyers Brigade*--Would find employment in dyeing our cloth, or the various sorts of thread we might require for the use of our weavers.

17. *The Dhobees Brigade*--Although among our community we should encourage every one to be his own dhobee, yet from the first we should have plenty of washing to employ a considerable number of hands.

18. *The Umbrella Makers Brigade*--Would find considerable scope in repairing the old frames collected by our Household Salvage Brigade; while the Sewing Brigade would work the covers.

19. *The Paper-makers Brigade*--Would also be supplied with plenty of material by the Household Salvage Brigade, and would keep our printing establishment supplied with whatever paper they might require. Already we consume a considerable quantity, and this would be enormously increased by the development of our scheme.

20. *The Book-binders Brigade*--Would furnish us with our registers for the Regimentation Bureau, besides doing our other miscellaneous work of a similar description.

21. *The Brass Brigade*--Would supply Our colonies with the various kinds of brazen vessels we should be likely to require. For these in process of time there would be a large demand.

22. *The Net-making Brigade*--Would make nets for fishing purposes.

33. *The Hawkers Brigade*--There could be no possible objection to our disposing of our goods in this way at the ordinary market rates supposing that we were in a position to manufacture more than we required for our own consumption.

24. *The Barbers Brigade*--Would also be a necessary addition to our forces, and would find plenty of scope for their skill among the unwashed multitudes who would compose our labour legions.

Such are some of the occupations which might at once be set on foot. To these would no doubt be added many other sorts of handicraft, as our numbers and experience increased, and fresh opportunities opened up around us.

CHAPTER VII.
SHELTER FOR ALL, OR THE HOUSING OF THE DESTITUTE.

A considerable portion of General Booth's book is devoted to the description of shelters, improved lodgings and suburban villages for the poor. As elsewhere remarked this question is not of such vital importance for India as for England, though the dealing with it is simply a question of time.

We would therefore simply refer our readers to the admirable proposals embodied in General Booth's book. It is possible that there may be some who will desire that immediate steps should be taken for the preparation of similar quarters for the poor in our terribly over-crowded Indian cities. It is in any case extremely likely that the question will be forced upon us at an early date by the people themselves.

But I have thought it best to narrow down the scheme as much as possible to those things which seem of the most absolute and immediate urgency, and I have therefore divested it as much as possible of all that could reasonably be dispensed with.

Still I see no reason why each city should not have its "Poor Man's Metropole," as well as its model dwellings and suburban villages, for the working classes. I would have these, moreover, as purely oriental as possible with a careful avoidance of anything that might be European in their appearance and arrangements. There should be tanks for bathing, and washing purposes, gardens, recreation grounds for the children, proper conveniences for cooking, and quarters in which they would not be herded together like cattle, but given the decencies of life, so necessary and helpful to the encouragement of cleanliness and morality.

Another point would be the absolute absence of anything in the shape of mere "charity" about any of the buildings. Everybody would be made to feel happy and at home, and their self-respect would be cultivated by arranging for suitable charges to be made, payment being taken either in cash or labour.

However, these are only hints that are thrown out, to show that we are fully awake to the importance of this subject, and in order that friends who are interested in the question may feel free to communicate their wishes and give us their advice.

CHAPTER VIII.
THE BEGGARS BRIGADE.

I now come to a special element of both hope and difficulty in the solution of our Indian Social problem,--The Beggars. Here we have the lowest stratum of the submerged tenth, excluding from them the religious mendicants with whom we are not now concerned. I have classified them as follows:--

1. The blind and infirm.
2. Those who help them and share the proceeds of their begging.
3. Able-bodied out of works.

Now I propose to deal with them in a way which will not call for Legislation. In the first place it is most improbable that Government would interfere with beggary, even if asked to do so. Certainly no such interference would be possible without assuming the responsibility of the entire pauper population, involving an expenditure of many million pounds. In the second place any such interference would in all likelihood be extremely distasteful to the native public. In the third place I believe the question can be better dealt with in another way.

I propose to cut diamond with diamond, to set a thief to catch a thief, to make a beggar mend a beggar. In other words my plan is to *reform* the system rather than *abolish* it. To the radical reformer who would sweep out the whole "nuisance" at one stroke, this may be a disappointment. But I believe that this feeling will be diminished, if not entirely removed, when he has made himself familiar with the following scheme.

Of course if the Upas tree could be uprooted and banished from our midst,--if with a wave of his magic wand some sorcerer could make it disappear, so much the better. But this is impossible. We should require an axe of gold to cut down the tree; and this we do not possess. If a rich and powerful Government shrinks from the expense of such an undertaking, we may well be excused for doing the same.

But after all supposing that you can transform your Upas tree into a fruit-bearing one, will not this be even better than to cut it down? Such things are done every day before our very eyes in nature. The stock of the crab-apple can be made to bear quinces, and a mango tree that is scarcely worth the ground it occupies, can be made to yield fruit which will fetch four annas a piece!

What is done in the garden is possible in human nature. And God will yet enable us to graft into this wretched and apparently worthless Upas stock, a bud which in coming years shall be loaded with fruit that shall be the marvel of the world. This human desert shall yet blossom as the rose, this wilderness shall become a fruitful garden, and the waste places be inhabited.

Surely then, better even than the ***annihilation*** of beggary will be its ***reformation***, should this be possible. At least the suggestion is well worthy of consideration, and in examining, the matter, there will be several important advantages to which I shall afterwards refer.

(1.) The first step that we would take in reforming the-beggars would be to ***regiment them.*** The task would be undertaken by our Labor Bureau. In this I do not think there would be serious difficulty encountered, if the scheme commended itself to the native public. They would only have to stop their supplies and send the beggars to us.

(2.) Our next step would be to ***sort out*** the beggars. They would be divided into three classes:--

(a) *The physically unfit*, who could be furnished with light work at our labor yards, or otherwise cared for. At present there are hundreds of beggars who are physically unfit for the exertion that begging involves, and who are driven to it by the desperate pangs of hunger.

(b) *Those who like* it, and are physically well fitted for it, besides being accustomed to the life, and not being fitted much for anything else.

(c) Those who dislike the life, and would prefer, or are suited for other occupations. Some of these we would draft off to other departments of our labour yards, while some would for the present be kept on as beggars, with the hope of early promotion to other employment.

(3.) We should ***brigade the beggars*** under the name of the Household Salvage Brigade, or some similar title, dividing them into small companies and appointing over them Sergeants from among themselves, and providing each with a badge or number.

(4.) We should with the advice and consent of the leading members of the native community, ***map out the city into wards***, and assign each company their respective streets, allotting as far as possible the Mahommedan beggars to the Mahommedan quarters, and the Hindoos to the Hindoo. In this we should also take the advice of experienced beggars, from whom we should expect to learn many useful hints.

(5,) Each house that was willing to receive them would ***be supplied with three receptacles***, one for waste cooked food, another for gifts of uncooked food, and a third for old clothes, waste paper, shoes, tins, bottles, and other similar articles.

(6.) At an appointed hour the Brigade would proceed to their posts, would patrol their wards, and bring or send the various articles collected to the labor yards, where all would be sorted and dealt with as necessary the cooked food being distributed among those who were willing to eat it, or sent to the surburban farm for our buffaloes. The raw grain would be handed over to our food depots, and credited by them to the Beggars Fund for the special benefit of the destitute.

(7.) At the end of each day every member of the Brigade would receive a food ticket in payment of his services. The amount could be regulated hereafter. This ticket he would present at our food depot, where he would be supplied with whatever articles he might require. There would be a regular system of rewards and encouragements for good conduct. But all such details will be settled hereafter.

(8.) A special feature in the system would be the introduction of the ancient ***Buddhist*** custom of "meetihal," or "the consecrated handful of rice." This is as follows. A pot is kept in each home and a handful of grain is put into it every time the family meal is cooked. We think that there would be no difficulty in getting this custom universally adopted, when it was understood that the proceeds would be devoted entirely to feeding the destitute. I believe that the income derived from this alone would in course of time be sufficient to meet the needs of the destitute in any city in India, at the same time that it would serve to equalise and therefore minimise the burden which now rests chiefly on a comparative few.

(9.) In case the food supply thus obtained should be insufficient, we have little doubt that we could persuade leading merchants in the city to club together and make up the difference, when they saw the good work that was going on.

Such in brief is a skeleton of the scheme for elevating and renovating the Beggar population of India. It is no doubt open to criticism on some points, but it has special advantages which I will proceed to point out, apologising for the extra space I am obliged to occupy, in dealing with this subject, on account of its novelty and importance, and in order that I may be thoroughly understood.

1. *It is conservative.* Here you have a reformation without a revolution, or rather a revolution by means of a reformation. And yet there is no attempted upheaval of society.

2. It is thoroughly *Indian*, and suited to the national taste.

3. It *costs nothing* and may even prove in time a source of income to the Social Scheme.

4. It is *doubly economical* since it uses the human waste in collecting what would be the natural wastage of the city, and devotes each to the service of the other.

5. It is *systematic* and therefore bound to be as immensely superior to the present haphazard mode, as a regular Army is to an undisciplined mob.

6. It unites the advantages of *moral suasion*, with those of the most perfect *religious equality* and *toleration.*

7. *It saves the State an enormous expenditure* and avoids the necessity for harsh, repressive, unpopular legislation, and increased taxation.

8. *It benefits the public.*

(a) It removes a public nuisance.

(b) And yet it satisfies the public conscience.

(c) It stimulates private charity, and directs its generosity into   wise   and beneficial channels.

9. ***It benefits the beggars.***

(a) It protects the weak from the painful and often unsuccessful   struggle for existence.

(b) It ensures everybody their daily food and a sufficiency of it.

(c) It restores their self respect.

(d) It teaches them habits of honesty, industry and thrift.

(e) It opens up to them a pathway of promotion.

10. Finally it will furnish honest and honorable employment right away for hundreds of thousands all over the land, and create an entirely *novel* industry out of what is at present an absolute *wreckage.*

But I am well aware that certain objections are likely to be raised. These I would seek to remove, though if we are to wait for a plan which is free from all liability to criticism, we may wait for ever, and wait in vain. There is a famous answer given by John Wesley to a lady who was objecting to something about his work,--"Madam, if there were a perfect organization in the world, it would cease to be so the day that you and I entered into it." Hence it is not simply a question as to whether there are difficulties in the present proposals, but can anything better be suggested. However, I am anxious to meet in the fairest possible manner all conceivable objections, and am perfectly prepared to make any such modifications as may appear advisable.

(1.) Some will perhaps say that the beggars are already too well off to desire to come,--that they are making a good thing of it and will prefer to prosecute their calling under the present arrangements. Of course if it be true that they are able to do better for themselves than we are proposing to do for them, then they have no right to be included in the submerged tenth. I would congratulate them on their success and turn my attention to those who are more in need of our services. But could any one seriously defend such a supposition? And if they are likely to be bettered by the new arrangements, why should we suppose that they should be so blind to their own interests as to refuse to profit by the new chance? Besides, this is contradicted by all experience. Let there be a prospect of a feast, or a supply of rice or food, and who does not know that beggars will flock eagerly to the point, though it be only for a single meal, and we propose to provide a *permanent livelihood.*

(2.) But says some one else ***they are bone-idle and will not work***, and you propose to give them no food save in exchange for their work. This is a real and serious difficulty. We fully recognise it. Yet we do not think it is un-get-over-able, for the following reasons:--

(a) We do not intend to be hard-taskmasters. The work given will be of a light character, and suited to the strength of each. We are not going in for oakum picking and stone breaking. We shall do our utmost to make everything bright, cheerful and easy. We have no idea of treating them as criminals.

(b) It ought not to be difficult to get each one to do two annas worth of work, and this will be more than sufficient to cover their expenses. We have no desire to become *sweaters.*

(c) *Begging is hard work.* If you don't believe it, come and try it! I and many of my officers have begged our food as religious mendicants, so that we, are able to speak from *experience*! It is at best a life of sacrifice, hardship and suffering. And yet we have practised it under *specially favorable circumstances*, particularly those of us who are Europeans. But that there can be any sort of rest, or ease, or enjoyment in it to those who are driven to it by the pangs of hunger, unsupported by any spiritual consolations, I cannot conceive. On the contrary I should say that the task of the beggar is so hard, and disagreeable not to say shameful, that the majority of them would leap to do the most menial tasks that would deliver them from a bondage so painful.

Have you ever solicited help and been refused? Have you known what it is to feel the awful sickenings of heart at hope deferred? Have you known what it is to be regarded with suspicion, with contempt, with dislike, with scorn, or even with *pity* by your fellow men? If so, you may be able to realise the experiences that every beggar has to go through a hundred times a day, many of them with feelings every bit as sensitive as your own. Will he demean himself and work hard at so miserable a calling and yet be unwilling to do some light work, with which he can earn an honest living? I for one cannot believe it, till I see it.

(d) Our experience further contradicts it in dealing with the more depraved, hardened and supposed-to-be-idle criminals and prostitutes, whom we receive into our Prison Gate and Rescue Homes. When Sir E. Noel Walker was visiting our Prisoners' Home in Colombo he was astonished at the *alacrity* with which the men obeyed orders, and the *eagerness* with which they worked at their allotted tasks. He asked the Officer in Charge whether he ever "hammered" them, and was surprised at finding that the only hammer he ever required was the *allsufficient* hammer of *love.* And yet the gates were always open and they were free to walk out whenever they liked. Moreover, beyond getting their food and a very humble sort of shelter, their labour was entirely unpaid.

(e) Finally by means of a judicious system of rewards and promotions we should educate and encourage them into working, besides teaching them industries which would be useful after they had left us.

(3.) But some one else will say "They are thievish and will rob you. They are roguish and will decieve you. You don't know whom you have to deal with." Well, if we don't know them, we should think nobody does! I would answer,

(a) Granted that some of them cheat us. All will not. And why should the honest suffer with the rogues?

(b) What if we do lose something in this way? It would be little in comparison with the enormous gain. I feel sure it would in no case exceed ten or twenty per cent, on the collections made, and that would be a mere trifle.

(c) Our system of regimentation would largely guard against any such danger and would be an encouragement to honesty.

(d) It is notorious that there is "honour among thieves." They would watch over one another. Among them "nimak-harami" or "faithlessness to their salt" would soon come to be regarded as a crime of the first water.

(e) The inducement for thieving would be largely gone. Very few steal *for the sake of stealing.* A man usually steals to fill his own stomach, or some one else's, whom he loves. But here all would be provided for.

(f) Besides he would feel that all he could earn was for the common good and was not going to make any individual rich at his expense.

(g) Our experience in the Prison Gate Homes contradicts it. True, we have had some thefts especially at the beginning, but when I was last visiting our Colombo Home, the Officers in charge assured me that they were now of the rarest occurrence, while the gentleman who owned the tempting cocoanuts that were hanging overhead told me that he had never had such good crops from his trees, as since our colony of thieves and criminals had been settled there!

(4.) Some one else may perhaps object that we shall have thrown upon our hands a swarm of helpless, useless, cripples and infirm. Well, and what if we do? Are they not our fellow human beings, and ought not some one to care for them? We shall look upon it as a precious responsibility, and I speak fearlessly on behalf of our devoted officers when I say, that they would rather spend and be spent for such than for the richest in the land. If, as I have already shown, the effort can be made *self-supporting* and *self-propagating*, the mere fact of their misery or poverty only impels us to love them the more and to strive the more earnestly for their emancipation.

CHAPTER IX.
THE PRISON GATE BRIGADE.

This has already been in operation for two years in the cities of Bombay and Colombo and a branch has been recently established in Madras. Now that it will be connected with other branches of our Social Reform, we may look for a rapid increase of this useful though difficult work.

The establishment of our Labor Yards will greatly help us in finding work for this class, without branding them with the perpetual stigma of their crime. The chief difficulty in the working of these Homes consists in the almost insuperable objection of the men to be **_known as criminals_** after their release from jail. This is of course perfectly natural. Besides, it is important that we should hold out before them hopes of bettering themselves by their good conduct, and earning an independent and honest livelihood at no distant date. When once our Labor Yards and Farm Colonies are in active operation, we shall be able to do this for our rescued criminals, continuing at the same time the fatherly supervision and help which they so very much need.

The following quotations from our last annual report will serve to explain this branch of our work, and to give a glimpse of the encouraging success with which we have already met in our efforts to reach and reform the criminal classes.

COLOMBO PRISON GATE HOME.

Picturesquely situated among palm trees in one of the most beautiful suburbs of Colombo, within easy reach of the principal city jail, is our Sinhalese Prisoners' Home. Cinnamon Gardens, as the district is called, forms one of the attractions of Colombo, which every passing visitor is bound to go and see. The beauty of the surroundings must be a pleasant contrast to those dull prison walls from which the inmates have just escaped. Still more blessed and cheering must be the change from the Warder's stern commands to the affectionate welcome and kindly attentions of the red-jacketed Salvationists, who have the management of the Home.

A bright lad who is on duty in the guard-room opens the gates and introduces you to the grounds in which the quarters are situated. There are groups of huts with mud walls and palm-leaf thatching, which have a thoroughly Indian and yet home like appearance. The first few of these are occupied as workshops or carpentry for the manufacture of tea boxes, and here from early to late the men may be seen busily employed, sawing, planing, measuring, bevelling, hammering and working with such a will that you might imagine their very lives depended on it, or at least that they must be making their fortunes out of it, whereas they are not being paid at all, and all the profits of the manufactory go towards the support of the Home!

"What I admire about your work," observed Sir Athur Gordon, the late Governor of Ceylon, "is the way in which your Officers identify themselves with these convicts, and live among them on terms of perfect equality."

But I was describing the little colony. On the left of this group of workshops is a neat little hut where Captain Dev Kumar and his young bride, Captain Deva Priti, reside. What a change for them form the English Homes to which they have been accustomed, to this little jungle hut, surrounded as they are continually by a band of ex-convicts, and criminals. Yet it would be hard to find a happier couple in the island,--in fact, quite impossible outside the Salvation Army.

"It is all our own work," explains the Captain. "Our men built the hut, and the materials only cost about Rs. 25!" Certainly this is the perfection of cheapness in the way of house building! A little further inside the enclosure you come to more huts, in some of which the men live, while others serve for quarters for the native officers who assist in the superintendence of the Home, and to whose noble efforts so much of its success is due. Then there is the kitchen, and a dining-room, and a stable for the bullock trap, in which the released prisoners are brought to the Home, to avoid the risk of a foot journey when their old associates might hinder them on the way.

The spare bits of ground are all laid out in little plots of garden, where plantains and vegetables are grown, and in front of the Captain's quarters is a dainty little scrap of a flower garden. The entire enclosure forms really a portion of the garden of a neighbouring house, the property of the late Mr. Ginger, who took a warm interest in our work, and leased the grounds to us at a nominal rent.

The following are the statistics of the work during the past year:--

Total number of admissions,	230
Found Situations,	115
Left, the Home and lost sight, of,	103
Total number of sentences of imprisonment	459
Number of juvenile convicts under 16 years of age,	40
Number of meals given,	5,774
Number of tea-boxes made, .	2,880
Profits on same,	Rs. 350

The accompanying is the official report form sent in by us to Government every month showing the results of the work--

JAIL GATE BRIGADE--COLOMBO--ITS RESULTS.

Prisons.

A.--This Return for the preceding month shall be forwarded on 1st or 2nd of each month, by the Officer Commanding Salvation Army, through the Superintendent of the Convict Establishment to the Inspector General of Prisons, with columns 1, 6, 7, and 8, duly filled in.

B.--The Superintendent Convict Establishment shall fill in columns 2, 3, 4, and 5, and send on the Return to the Inspector General.

1. Name and age of Prisoner.

2. Nationality and religion.

3. Name of Offence.

4. Length of imprisonment in months.

5. General character in Jail.

6. Number of days maintained by the Salvation Army

7. How employed now, or going to be employed.

8. Result of action of salvation Army on prisoner, roughly estimated.

Superintendent Convict Establishment.

Commdt. Salvation Army, Colombo.

That the work of the Colombo Prisoners' Home is highly appreciated in Colombo is further proved by the fact that most of the leading Government officials subscribe to its funds, including the Colonial Secretary, Sir E. Noel Walker, the Chief Justice Sir Bruce Burnside, and many others. Again, it is not an uncommon thing for us to receive such letters as the following from the Magistrate:--

From the POLICE MAGISTRATE, Colombo,
To the CAPTAIN OF THE PRISON GATE BRIGADE.
Dated, Colombo, October 30th, 1889.

Subject--Habitual Offender, Dana.

Sir,

I have the honour to inform you that a man named Dana, produced before me this day, charged with being a habitual thief, has expressed a wish to be admitted into the Prison Brigade Home.

I shall be glad if you afford him an opportunity to redeem his character.

I am, Sir,
Your obedient Servant,
E.W.M.,
Police Magistrate.

The past year was suitably finished up by providing a special feast to which only ex-convicts were admitted. No less than 150 accepted the invitation.

About this branch of our work a leading daily paper, the Ceylon *Independent*, writes as follows.--

Most of our readers have read in our columns of the good work the

Army is doing at the Prison Gate, in reclaiming from criminal courses the discharged prisoners who have served their time of confinement. In that critical moment, when the wide world is once more before the newly discharged culprit, when he emerges from confinement to overwhelming temptation, big it may be with fresh schemes of crime, armed with enlarged experiences to aid in its accomplishment, to be met, taken kindly by the hand, and led gently to the pleasanter and more peaceful path of honesty, industry, and virtue, is a surprise that is calculated to disarm temptation at least for a moment, and thus virtue gains time for thought.

The success of the Prison Gate Brigade has hitherto been surprising, and quite beyond its founders' anticipation. It has been especially useful in reclaiming juvenile offenders, of whom a large number have been induced to take to the honest means of livelihood, chiefly carpentry, which the Home provides.

OUR BOMBAY PRISON GATE BRIGADE.

This work in Bombay was commenced some two years ago at the instance of a leading Parsee gentleman, with a generous subscription of Rs. 1,200. Owing partly to the fact that we have been hitherto unable to secure suitable premises and partly to the entire absence of any assistance on the part of Government, the work in Bombay has been much more uphill and discouraging than in Ceylon. Nevertheless we have persevered in the teeth of all sorts of difficulties, and the results have been very encouraging. Recently in one week no less than three of the inmates of our Bombay Home were accepted as cadets, to be trained up as future officers. Previously to this nine others had been similarly accepted. One of these, Lieut. Hira Singh, is now himself taking an active part in the rescue of other convicts, while another is sucessfully working in Gujarat. Accounts of their lives are given further on.

Indeed Bombay has proved itself to be an even richer field than Colombo itself; and now that some of the peculiar difficulties that have hitherto hindered the work, are one by one being removed, there is every reason to believe that this work will soon make rapid progress.

The returns for the past year show that the prison gates have been visited 235 times, for the purpose of meeting the convicts on their release. Since the commencement of the Home about 134 men have been admitted. Of these 74 have professed conversion, about 12 having been accepted as officers by ourselves and the remainder having mostly found employment elsewhere. The number of meals given during the past year has been about 7,800.

One of the special features of the work here consists in the constant visitation of the liquor dens, with a view to persuading those who were frequenting them to give up their evil ways. No less than 430 such were in this way visited and a large number of papers distributed. While the opposition was in some instances severe, as a rule our officers were well treated even by the grogshop-keepers, who while admitting that their trade was evil, pleaded that they had the Government's approval, and that they must somehow support themselves and their families.

Besides the regular inmates, a large number of casuals have been relieved and assisted, but of these we have no exact figures.

The following are some specimens of the work done by us among the criminal classes in Bombay and Ceylon:--

LIEUTENANT HIRA SINGH

Is a Hindu of the Kshatraya caste. He comes of a soldier race and family, his father having served in the East India Company's army before him, and he having from his youth followed the same profession for the past eighteen years, serving successively as Private, Lance-Corporal, Corporal, and Sergeant in a native Regiment. He went through the last Afghan campaign, having been to Cabul, Quetta, and other places.

For many years his conduct was excellent, but latterly he took to drinking, got into serious trouble with the police, and was sent to prison for forty days, thus losing his post as well as his claim to pension. He was met by our officers on his release, accompanied them to the Home, gave his heart to God, and has now been an officer in our ranks for more than a year. During most of this time he has been connected with our Bombay Prison Gate work, and has in turn helped to rescue many others. But for the help he then received, a life of drunkenness and crime would probably have been, almost forced upon him. He is a good specimen of numbers who would *like* to reform, but with ruined reputation have no choice, save between starvation and crime.

HARMANIS.

"I am a native (Singhalese) of Kalutara in Ceylon. My father was a toddy-drawer. We were very poor. Sometimes my uncles would give me a cent or two for mounting guard to give them warning about anybody's approach while they were slaughtering stolen cattle in the jungles. Once, being very hungry, I climbed up a palm tree to steal cocoanuts, but was caught by the owner and handed over to the police. The magistrate sent me to jail for three weeks. After my release I came to Colombo, and falling in with the Salvation Army, I went to their Home for prisoners, and now thank God I am saved."

PODI SINGHA

This is only one of the many aliases by which he is known. He has been one of the worst thieves and bad characters to be met with even in Colombo, where there is a pretty good assortment of the scum of slumdom. Adopted as an infant by a pious Mahomedan, he was trained up in that religion. But in spite of every effort that was made for his reformation, he rapidly went from bad to worse, till at length he found himself in the hands of the police.

His first sentence was twelve months for throwing sand in a Singhalese man's eyes and then robbing him of his comb. When released he fell in with other criminals, from whom he learnt many new tricks of the trade. Once he was stealing some clothes from a line when the lady of the house saw him. A hue and cry was raised, and he soon found himself surrounded with coolies and dogs. Seeing that there was no chance of escape, he began to jump and scream and go through all sorts of antics.

The lady, thinking he was mad, and having pity on him, let him go.

He has seen the inside of nearly all the Colombo jails, but without being made any better. Finally, he was received into our Home. At first he was rather troublesome, but after a short time he gave his heart to God, and has been doing well. "He cannot read or write," says the Captain in charge, "but he prays like a divine, and I am believing to see him become an Officer some day."

JANIS

Was brought from his village by a Singhalese gentleman when quite a little boy, but, leaving his master, thought he would start life on his own account. He soon became a practised thief. "I always managed to escape," he says, "till one day with some of my companions I robbed a Buddhist temple. I managed to get a silver 'patara' (plate), which we sold for Rs. 24, but was caught and sent to jail." "But you were yourself a Buddhist," said the Captain. "How came you to rob your own temple?" "What of that? I thought nothing of sin in those days. But it is all so different now. I am saved, and mean to spend all my life in saving others. I am just now practising a song to sing in the meeting to-night."

The Captain asked him whether he did not think it a great disgrace to go to jail. "Oh, no! I thought everybody in Colombo had been there some time or other. All the people with whom I mixed had been." "Well, how did you like it?" "Oh, it was not such a bad place! The food was fairly good, and I had not to work very hard but I wish I had known about salvation sooner. Even then I used to wish that I could find something which would *make* me good, but all my efforts were in vain till I came to the Home, and got saved."

In conclusion, I feel sure that a few brief particulars regarding this branch of our work in Australia will be read with interest, and will serve to prove the usefulness of this portion of our social reform scheme:

Some six or seven, Prisoners' Homes have been established in Australasia. The Victorian Government give an annual grant of L1,000, to assist us in this branch of our work. Special facilities are afforded to our Officers in visiting the prisoners, and in some of the jails printed notices are posted up by the authorities to the effect that any prisoner, previous to discharge, may communicate with the officers in charge of our Home, with a view to making a fresh start in life.

The testimony of Sir Graham Berry, Agent General, the Chief Secretary, the Inspector General of Penal Establishments, and the Chief Commissioner of Police, proves conclusively how much good has thus been done. The following extracts from their letters are copied from our Australasian Prison Gate report:--

H.E. SIR H.B. LOCH, K.C.B., G.C.M.G., writes through his Private Secretary to express "his approval and appreciation of the work done by the Salvation Army in connection with the Prison Gate Brigades and Rescued Sisters' Homes, and has great pleasure in expressing his belief in the good which has resulted from the philanthrophic endeavours of the Salvation Army to rescue and afford material assistance to those in whose interests these organisations have been formed."

SIR GRAHAM BERRY, Agent General for Victoria, writes:--"I have confidence in the permanent results of your labours, because you, treat these unfortunates as if they were human beings and capable of better things. I believe your organisation is a very powerful agency for good among that class which is practically neglected by others."

CHIEF JUSTICE HIGGINBOTHAM says that "it is only proper to mention that there is no better nor more useful work done in rescuing discharged prisoners from relapsing into crime, than that effected by the Prison Gate Brigade of the Salvation Army."

Similar letters have also been received from the following gentlemen:--

The Hon. ALFRED DEAKIN, M.L.A., Chief Secretary.
The Hon. JAMES BALFOUR, M.L.C.
The Hon. M.H. DAVIES, M.L.A. (Speaker of the Legislative Assembly).
The Hon. F.F. DERHAM, M.L.A., Postmaster General.
The Hon. H.T. WRIXON, M.L.A., Attorney General.
The Hon. W.F. WALKER, M.L.A., Commissioner of Customs.
Mr. JUSTICE KERFERD.
The Bishop of MELBOURNE.
W.G. BRETT, Esq., Inspector General, Penal Department.
H.M. CHOMLEY, Esq., Chief Commissioner of Police.
A. SHIELDS, Esq., M.P., Medical Officer, Melbourne Jail.

CHAPTER X.
THE DRUNKARD'S BRIGADE.

Hundreds of habitual drunkards have been soundly converted and reformed in connection with our ordinary spiritual work in India. Probably there are not less than 500 such enrolled in our ranks in this country, and turned into staunch and perpetual abstainers.

The terrible nature of the drinks and drugs consumed by the Natives, I have already had occasion to describe, as also the increasingly large number of those who are becoming enchained by the habit.

In connection with our present Social Reform, special efforts will be made to reach this class. They will be personally dealt with, and placed as far as possible in circumstances that shall put them beyond the reach of their besetting temptation.

For some time past our Officers, more especially those in charge of the Prison Gate work, have visited liquor-shops and opium and ganja dens, speaking personally to the frequenters, and in some cases distributing among them suitable appeals and warnings in regard to the fatal consequences of the habit.

Untimately it is intended to establish homes for the most hopeless class of inebriates, both for those habituated to liquor and for those who are the slaves of the still more fatal drugs, such as opium and bhang.

CHAPTER XI.
THE RESCUE HOMES FOR THE FALLEN.

Here again we have made a beginning. It is now a year since the opening of our Home in Colombo, and during that time 52 girls have been received into our Home. Of these

    2 have been restored to their friends,

    4 are with others--doing well,

    23 have turned out unsatisfactory, and

    23 are with us in the Home, almost without exception giving evidence of being truly reformed.

Heart-rending are the tales which have reached our ears as to the way in which many of them have been decoyed from their homes, and as to the miserable existence which they have since been dragging out.

Every Indian city teems with a too fast increasing number of similar unfortunates, for whom at present nothing has been attempted. We propose, therefore, very largely to extend our Homes at all the large centres of population.

Connected as will be this department with the network of other agencies that we have already established, and increased as will be our facilities for reaching this class, we are confident that we shall be able to carry out this much-needed reform on a scale commensurate with the evil, besides warning the youths of our cities against the terrible contamination to which they are at present exposed. All the weight of our increasing influence will be thrown into the scale for cutting off both the supply and demand of this infamous traffic in human souls.

CHAPTER XII.
"THE COUNTRY COLONY"--"WASTEWARD HO!"

As has been already explained in the first part of this book, the congested state of the labor market in the agricultural districts is leading to an enormous and increasing immigration of the country population towards the towns, not as a matter of preference, or of choice, but of dire necessity. The object of the Country Colony, as applied to India, will be twofold:

1. It will seek to divert into more profitable channels the steadily increasing torrent of immigration from the villages to the towns.

2. It will re-direct and re-distribute the masses of the Submerged Tenth who already exist in every large city.

Like his English representative, the Indian village bumpkin has a natural aversion to town life. Peculiarities in his dialect, dress, and manners make him the laughing-stock of the clever Cockney townsman. His simplicity and ignorance of the world cause him to be easily victimised by the city sharper, for whom he is no match in the struggle of life. He sighs for his green fields, and longs to get away from the bustle that everywhere surrounds and bewilders him. He surrenders these preferences only, because starvation is staring him in the face, and he has better chances of working, begging, or stealing in the city than in his village.

And yet within a few miles of his birthplace there are frequently tracts of waste land amply sufficient to support him and thousands more. He could reduce it to cultivation if he had the chance. He would infinitely prefer eking out the scantiest existence in this manner to flinging himself into the turbulent whirlpool of town life. Strangely enough the "Sirkar" (Government), to whom these tracts belong, is equally anxious that the land in question should be cultivated. It would yield in the course of a few years as rich a revenue as the acres of exactly similar soil that have been brought under cultivation in the neighbourhood. But the difficulties in the way are well nigh insuperable:

1. The congested labor consists almost entirely of those castes which are looked upon as inferior. The very idea of their emancipation is distasteful to the higher castes, who enjoy in most parts of India an almost exclusive monopoly of the land. Hence any effort to obtain a grant of waste land is met with strong and often bitter opposition, and it is next door to impossible for any one in the position of the Submerged Tenth to fight the battle through.

2. Of course, under the British Government these caste distinctions are not officially recognised. But as a matter of fact they still carry great weight. Anybody can, it is true, petition the Government for a grant of this land, but to secure favourable consideration is almost impossible. During the last four or five years I have personally interested myself in several petitions, with a view to assisting the petitioners, whom I knew to be thoroughly deserving of success. And yet after going through a weary tissue of formalities, seldom lasting less than a year, I have not known of a single favourable answer, nor have these advances met with the least sort of encouragement. The Government officials to whom these vast estates are entrusted are mostly so preoccupied with other work that it is impossible for them to give to the subject the personal attention that it requires, and they are guided by the reports of interested and sometimes bribed subordinates. The very fact that they are entitled to draw exactly the same salary whether the public estate improves or not, removes the incentive that would otherwise exist, even if they were the absentee landlords of the property, while the constant liability to be transferred from one district to another aggravates the difficulty of the situation.

3. Again, there is a lack of the capital necessary for the initial expenses of the cultivator in sinking wells, building houses, supplying cattle and obtaining both seed and food till the harvest has been gathered in.

4. The lack of combination among the congested mass of labourers is another serious evil. They are as sheep without a shepherd. Individually they have no influence. Collectively they are capable of becoming a mighty power. What is needed at the present moment is a directing head and an enfolding organisation that shall gather them together, bind them in one harmonious whole, and with the help of a friendly Government lead them on to occupy and cultivate these waste lands,

converting them into districts inhabited by a sober, thrifty and enterprising population. Without such a combination the efforts that are made by private enterprise will continue to be carried out on such a petty scale as will utterly fail to cope with or remove the existing evil, and will merely serve to give relief in a few isolated cases. For instance I have in mind one district where to my personal knowledge the amount of congested labor cannot amount on the most moderate calculation to less than half a million people. There is in their immediate neighbourhood abundance of waste land capable of supporting them. The Government is anxious for that land to be occupied. The people are eager to obtain and capable of cultivating every piece of waste that can be placed at their disposal. If, instead of leaving it to individual caprice and effort to carry on in the present haphazard and redtape fashion, we are able on the one hand to combine this mass of labor, and to obtain on the other hand from Government the particulars of the land they are desirous of having cultivated, and the most favorable terms on which it can be granted to us, we shall be in a position with, but a very moderate amount of capital at our command, to solve the double problem of the waste land and waste labor, and that within a very short period.

5. The religious influences which we should bring to bear on the colonists would be invaluable, especially in the early days of these colonies. The example of our Officers, their self-sacrificing devotion to the interests of the people, the knowledge that they would gain nothing by the success of the enterprise and that they were actuated solely by the highest motives, the facts that they were sharing the homes of the people, enduring the same hardships and eating the same food, all this would act as an inspiration to the colonists when the early days of trial and difficulty came upon them. No less an authority than Mr. John Morley, M.P., remarked when he first heard of General Booth's scheme, that he considered that its combination of religion with the other details of the plan of campaign was its most hopeful feature, and would be most likely to ensure its success. This seems to apply especially to that portion of the scheme now under consideration. Indeed, were such an enterprise directed solely by an agency destitute of this powerful lever, we should anticipate failure in nine cases out of ten, no matter how great the ability that directed and how abundant the capital that could be commanded. Individual rapacity and selfishness would spoil everything, and instead of a beautiful spirit of

harmony and self-sacrifice, we should find a lucky few gaining the prizes and the masses left no better, perhaps worse, off than before.

With these preliminary remarks I would introduce the Country Colony, as suggested by General Booth. It will consist of the following branches, to which no doubt others will be added as we advance:--

1. The Suburban Farm in the vicinity of large cities, including
   (a) A dairy for the supply of milk, ghee, cream and butter.
   (b) A market garden for fruit and vegetables.
2. The Industrial Village.
3. The Social Territory or Poor Man's Paradise.
4. The City of Refuge.
5. Miscellaneous:
   (a) Gangs for public works, such as tanks, railways, roads, &c.
   (b) Gangs for tea gardens.
   (c) Land along the railways.

CHAPTER XIII.
THE SUBURBAN FARM.

The connecting link between the City Colony and the Country Colony will be the Suburban Farm. Situated conveniently near to the largest cities, it will serve many important purposes.

1. It will form the channel, or outlet, by which the agricultural portion of the labor overflow in the cities will make its way back to the country. In fact, it will constitute a sort of sluice which will in time act with the same regularity and ease as those which are attached to any reservoir of water, directing to the most needy places, and distributing without waste, those very waters which if uncontrolled would sweep everything before them as a devastating flood.

2. It will at the same time find a ready market in the city, not only for its own produce, but for that of the other branches of the country colony, with which it would be in constant and close communication.

3. It will supply the city with wholesome and unadulterated dairy produce, together with the best fruits and vegetables, at the ordinary market rates. These could be disposed of either wholesale to city merchants, or by moans of stalls in the various markets, or we could undertake to retail them in connection with our Household Salvage Brigade. The Suburban Farm would consist of, say, from fifty to five hundred acres of land in the immediate neighbourhood of a city. It would combine three or more separate departments.

1. *The Dairy.* Buffaloes and cows would be given us by friends, besides being purchased and reared by us, in large numbers. To tend them, milk them, prepare the ghee, cream and butter, and to convey it all to town, would find employment for a large number of the Submerged Tenth.

2. The ***Market Garden*** would employ a still larger number. Bananas grow

quickly in all parts of India, and with them we could make an immediate beginning, introducing from different districts the best species. Sugar-cane and other popular native products would receive special attention, and where the European population in the neighbourhood was sufficiently numerous we could include the cultivation of such fruits and vegetables as would be liked by them. In the case of seaport towns we should no doubt do a large business with the steamers in the harbour, as for instance, in Bombay, Colombo, or Calcutta.

3. We should probably at an early period transfer some of the industrial brigades enumerated in Chapter VI to our Suburban Farm. In doing this there would be several obvious advantages:

(a) We should have more elbow room for them on the Farm, than in the Labor Yards, where land would be so expensive that we should be obliged to crowd everything into the smallest possible compass, both in regard to work sheds and sleeping accommodation.

(b) In removing them from the contaminating influences of city life, we should be able to exercise a more personal and powerful influence upon these members of the Submerged Tenth and should stand a far better chance of effectively carrying out that spiritual and moral regeneration, without which we reckon that any mere temporal reformation would be ineffective and evanescent.

(c) We should prevent our labor yards from getting gorged, and would keep them within manageable dimensions. At the same time that we should cope more effectively with all existing distress.

(d) The Suburban Farm being closely connected with other portions of our Country Colony, we should be able to use the latter to relieve it in case of its becoming in turn overcrowded by the influx from the City.

(e) It would thus form a natural stepping-stone to the Industrial Village, which we have next to describe.

CHAPTER XIV.
THE INDUSTRIAL VILLAGE.

For the Industrial Village we have already before our very eyes an admirable object lesson in the existing organisation and subdivision of an ordinary Indian village. Indeed it is singular how precisely India has anticipated just what General Booth now proposes to introduce in civilized Europe.

The village community so familiar to all who have resided in India consists of an independent or rather interdependent, co-operative association which constitutes a miniature world of its own, producing its own food and manufacturing its own clothes, shoes, earthenware, pots, &c, with its own petty government to decide all matters affecting the general welfare of the little commonwealth. Very wisely the British rulers of India have left this interesting relic of ancient times untouched, so that the institution can be seen in complete working order at the present day all over India. The onward march of civilisation has somewhat shaken the fabric and has threatened the existence of several of the village industries. But at present there has not been any radical alteration. The village may still be seen divided up into its various quarters.

Take for instance a village in Gujarat. Those substantial houses in the centre belong to the well-to-do landowners. The cultivators or tenants have their quarters close alongside. The group of huts belonging to the weavers is easily distinguishable by the rude looms and apparatus for the manufacture of the common country cloth. The tanners' quarter is equally well marked, and yonder the groups at work with mud and wheel and surrounded with earthenware vessels of various shapes and sizes, remind you that you are among the Potters.

On inquiring into the interior economy of the village a system of payment in kind and exchange of goods for labour and grain is found to prevail exactly similar to that suggested by General Booth. Only here we have the immense advantage that instead of having to explain and institute a radical reform in the existing system, we have to deal with millions of people who are thoroughly imbued with these principles from their infancy.

For instance one of the staple articles of food in the village consists of buttermilk, which is distributed by the high caste among the low caste from year's end to year's end in return for petty services. One of the usual ways in which the high caste will punish the low, for any course of conduct to which they object is by the terrible threat of stopping their supply of "chas," which means usually nothing short of starvation.

Here then is our model in good working order and in exact accordance with the ideal sketched out by General Booth. We cannot do better than adhere to it as closely as possible.

Probably the first industrial settlement which we shall establish, in addition to the labor yards and suburban farms already referred to, will consist of a colony of Weavers in Gujarat.

For this we shall have special facilities, as we have now 150 Officers at work in that part of the country, as well as more than 2,000 enrolled adults, a large proportion of whom have been in our ranks for several years. From amongst these we shall be able to select thoroughly reliable superintendents (both European and Native), and shall be able to take full advantage of their local experience.

But how far we shall consider it wise to confine our first settlement to one particular caste or to include within it from the outset some other useful village industries such as have been above referred to, I am not as yet prepared to say. Much will necessarily depend on the course that events may hereafter take. For the present I can only say that we will adhere as closely as possible to our Indian model.

The one weak point about the Indian system, as it at present exists, is, that there is no means of regulating the proportion of labour in each section of the community. The rules of caste prevent any transfer from one trade to another, while there is no system of intercommunication between the villages to enable them to readily transfer their surplus population to the places where they would be most needed. In a case where some village industry is threatened with annihilation, as for instance the weavers, there is absolutely no provision for the transfer of the unfortunate victims of civilisation either to some more favored locality or to some other sphere of labour.

Now this is just where our combined plan of campaign with its union of City, Country, and Over-sea Colonies would step in and supply the missing link. We should be able to direct the glut of labor into just those channels where it would be the most useful.

And why should this be thought impracticable? Everybody is acquainted with the power of wind, water and steam, where properly directed, to move the most gigantic machinery and yet for centuries those powers were suffered to go to waste. It is only of late that we have learnt for instance to put chains upon the genii of the tea-kettle, to put them as it were into harness, to bridle them and to compel them to drag our huge leviathans across thousands of miles of ocean. May not the enormous mass of waste labor that has accumulated in our cities and rural districts be fitly compared to the former waste of steam. The best that we have been able to do for it so far has been to provide for it the safety valves of beggary, destitution, famine, pestilence, crime, imprisonment and the gallows.

Is it too much to suppose that this enormous waste of human steam, the most valuable sort of steam that the world contains, can be properly controlled and guided so that it will make for itself railways and steamers that shall carry its human cargoes by millions across lands that are at present mere wastes, and to populate countries which are as yet wildernesses? In doing so, we shall but fulfil the words of prophecy uttered 26,000 years ago. "The wilderness and the solitary place shall be glad for them, and the desert shall rejoice and blossom as the rose. It shall blossom abundantly, and rejoice even with joy and singing.* * For in the wilderness shall waters break out and streams in the desert. And the parched ground shall become a pool and the thirsty land springs of water.* * * And an highway shall be there, and a way, and it shall be called the way of holiness; the unclean shall not pass over it, but it shall be for those. The way-faring men, though fools shall not err therein. No lion shall be there, nor any ravenous beast shall go up thereon; it shall not be found there. But the redeemed shall walk there, and the ransomed of the Lord shall return and come to Sion with songs and everlasting joy upon their heads. They shall obtain joy and gladness, and sorrow and sighing shall flee away."

CHAPTER XV.
THE SOCIAL TERRITORY, OR, POOR MAN'S PARADISE.

Probably the biggest wholesale emigration scheme ever undertaken was that of Israel out of Egypt into Canaan, under the leadership of Moses. The circumstances were so very similar to those with which we are dealing, that I may be excused for referring to them, as they have a direct bearing on the present problem, and may help largely towards its solution. It is said that "History repeats itself" and certainly this is true in regard to the evils that then existed, and we do not see why the remedy should not in some respect correspond.

Looking back then, we find that there was in Egypt in the year 1,500 B.C. a submerged tenth, consisting of 600,000 able-bodied men with their wives and families and numbering therefore at least two and a half million souls. They constituted a distinct caste, or nation, which had been grafted into the original Egyptian stock 430 years previously. Owing to hereditary customs, race distinctions and religious differences they had preserved their identity and had never become assimulated with the Egyptians. It was a famine that had driven them to take refuge in Egypt at a time when their numbers were so few that their presence caused no particular inconvenience to the original inhabitants, while the services of the King's Vazir, to whose caste they belonged secured them a suitable reception.

At the time however when we take up their history a change had taken place. Their numbers had immensely increased. The labor market was deluged with them. The rulers, capitalists and landowners began to tremble for their very existence. Enormous public works were planned and the enslaved caste were compelled to carry out their allotted labour under rigorous taskmasters, who made their lives a burden to them. Still their numbers continued to increase. Alarmed at the prospect of an impending revolution, the King gave orders that every male child of the Hebrews should be drowned, thinking thus to stamp out the nation. It is easy to imagine therefore that affairs must have come to a desperate pass, when from the palace of Pharaoh and yet from among their own caste a deliverer was raised up to organise and carry out the wholesale emigration of the entire nation.

Looked at in this light it was certainly the boldest venture and greatest scheme of the kind that had ever been conceived, and without the aid of remarkable miraculous displays of Divine power Moses could never have carried out so magnificent a project.

Everything appeared to be against him. The people whom he had come to deliver were an undisciplined mob of cowardly slaves, whose spirit had been crushed by years of cruel tyranny. They were unarmed and unaccustomed to war. They were the subjects of the most powerful military monarchy of those times. For them to dream of emigrating must have seemed the wildest folly. On the one hand the Egyptians would not hear of it, and their way would be barred by legions of the best soldiers the world could produce. On the other hand the country to which they were to emigrate was already occupied by numerous and warlike tribes, who would contest every inch of territory. Added to this there was a "great and howling wilderness" which separated the one country from the other.

Hence it will be seen that this vast national emigration scheme was carried out by Moses under circumstances of peculiar difficulty which do not exist in the problem at present under consideration.

There are the same destitute hunger-bitten multitudes, it is true, and the same difficulty arises before us as to what to do with these steadily increasing hordes. The same Egyptian remedy, the construction of vast public works, has been resorted to over and over again, with the effect of giving temporary, but not permanent relief. In some respects the position of the Hebrews in Egypt was preferable to that of the destitute masses in India. They seem at least to have had no lack of food and shelter, and if they had to work hard, and were cruelly treated by their taskmasters, we have become familiar in the Indian villages with many instances of cruelty in the treatment of the low caste by the high such as could not well have been surpassed in Egypt itself, to say nothing of the extortions of the money-lender and the ravages of famine and pestilence referred to elsewhere.

But in many respects the situation is far more hopeful. Our Pharaoh is a Christian Queen, under whom we have, not one, but many Josephs, who are really anxious for the highest welfare of the submerged masses, and who are likely to hail with gladness (as has been already the case in England) any project which bids fair to alleviate permanently the existing misery. The wealth and power of the British Government and Nation, instead of being used to hinder such a scheme, is likely to be thrown bodily into the scale in favour of all reasonable reform that will help congested labour to redistribute itself and recover its normal balances.

Again the progress of science and civilization has removed immense barriers that previously existed, and railways, steamers, post and telegraph have rendered possible for us, if not comparatively easy, what was before only within the reach of miraculous manifestations of Divine Power.

Furthermore, ***the land is there, plenty of it, for centuries to come***, some of it across the seas, within easy reach of our steamers, but a great deal of it quite close at hand. Nor will it be necessary to dispossess others to occupy it. The only enemies that will have to be faced are the wild beasts, always ready to beat a retreat when man appears. It does not even belong to some different nationality or Government, jealous of our encroachments, but is the property of the same Power to whom these destitute multitudes are looking for their daily bread.

Hence it is impossible to imagine circumstances more favorable than those which already exist in India at the moment that General Booth's scheme is placed before the public, towards the carrying out on an enormous scale, hitherto never dreamt of, the portion of his projects referred to in the present chapter.

What I would propose is that a considerable section of waste Territory should be assigned to us and placed at our disposal in some suitable part of India, upon which we could plant colonies of the destitute, similar in many respects to those already described, save that we should here carry out on a wholesale scale what elsewhere we should be doing by retail. Into this central lake or reservoir all our scattered streams would empty themselves, till it was so far full that we should require to repeat the process elsewhere. Beginning with a single social reservation in some specially selected district, we should easily be able to repeat the experiment elsewhere on an even larger scale profiting as we went along by our accumulated experience.

From the first, however, I should suppose that it would be preferable to carry out the manoeuvre on as large a scale as possible, for the reason that this is just one of those things which will be found easier to do wholesale than retail.

We have many illustrations of this in business. The merchant who amasses a colossal fortune will perhaps scarcely spend an hour a day in superintending the working of an establishment that covers half an acre, while the poor retail shop-keeper over the way toils from early morning to late at night and is scarcely able then to earn a bare subsistence for the support of his family.

Compare again the labour and profits of a boatman in Bombay Harbour, with those of the owner of an ocean going steamer. The former toils day and night at the peril of his life and earns but little, while the latter rests comfortably at home and enjoys a handsome income.

Or again let the village hand-loom weaver be pitted against the Bombay Mill-owner, and we see at a glance that under certain circumstances it *pays* infinitely better to do things on a large than on a small scale, and that in so doing the amount of labour and risk are also economised.

Now this applies to the proposal contained in this chapter. Given a people who are well acquainted with Indian agriculture and who are willing to be moved;-- given a leader and an organisation in which they have confidence;--given those religious and moral influences which will so help them in overcoming the initial difficulties of the enterprise; and given a suitable tract of country which (without displacing existing population) they can occupy, and I would say with confidence that it will be found easier to accomplish the transfer on a large than on a small scale, by wholesale rather than by retail.

In the present case all the above conditions are satisfied. The entire congested labor of the rural districts is thoroughly versed from childhood in the arts of Indian agriculture. They are willing in many parts of the country to emigrate by thousands even across the "kala pani," to which they have such an intense and religious aversion, or to enlist by thousands in our merchant marine and military forces. Much more then will they be willing to emigrate in far larger numbers to districts close at hand. A leader to inspire, an organisation to enfold, and a plan of campaign to guide, have in the most marvellous manner almost dropped from the skies since the publication of General Booth's book. The religious and moral restraints and incentives, so important for guarding against the abuses of selfishness and for inspiring with a spirit of cheerful self-sacrifice, are provided, and that in a purely *Native garb*, and yet with all the advantages of European leadership and enthusiasm. And finally there is land in abundance which Government desires to see colonised, and which is being slowly retailed out bit by bit in a manner altogether unworthy of the urgent necessities of the occasion.

What then is there to hinder a big bold experiment? General Booth will have in England largely to *make* his agriculturists before he can put them upon the land. Here in India we have *millions* of skilled destitutes ready to hand, and it will be possible within a very short period with a few bold strokes to relieve the congested labor market from one end of India to the other in a manner that can hardly now be conceived.

Is not this plan infinitely superior to the spasmodic Egyptian expedient of occasional public works, which cost the State enormous sums and only increase the local difficulty as soon as they are completed? Should we not here be erecting a satisfactory and permanent bulwark against the future inroads of famine? Shall we not rather be increasing the public revenue for future years by millions of pounds and that without adding a single new tax, or relying upon sources so uncertain and detrimental to the public welfare as those founded upon the consumption of drugs and liquors that destroy the health of the people? Shall we not again be increasing the stability and glory of the Empire in caring for its destitute masses and in turning what is now a danger to the State into a peaceful, prosperous and contented community? And finally will not our Poor Man's Paradise be infinitely superior from every point of view to the miserable regulation *workhouse*, that is in other countries offered by the State, or again to the system of charitable doles and wholesale beggary that at present exists? To me it seems that there is indeed no comparison between the two, and General Booth's book has opened out a vista of happiness to the poor, such as we should hardly have conceived possible save in connection with a Christian millennium or a Hindoo "Kal Yug."

But it may be objected by some that in providing those outlets for the destitute, we should in the end only aggravate the difficulty by enormously increasing the population. This reminds one of the gigantic folly of the miser with his hoards of gold. An amusing eastern anecdote is told of one who having gone two or three miles to say his prayers to a mosque suddenly remembered that he had forgotten to put out an oil lamp before leaving home. He at once retraced his steps and on reaching his house called out to the servant girl to be sure and put out the light. She replied that she had already done so, and that it was a pity he had wasted his shoe leather in walking back so far to remind her. To this he answered that he had already thought of this and had therefore taken off his shoes and carried them under his arm so as not to wear them out!

And here you have a wretched class of miserly so-called "economists" who are afraid to light their lamp, lest they should burn the oil, and who would rather sleep in the darkness, doing nothing, or break their necks fumbling about in their vain efforts to do little, when for a farthing dip they may put in hours of profitable toil! And when a shoe is provided for the swollen foot of a nation they are so afraid of wasting their shoe leather, that they would rather hobble about belamed with thorns, stones, heat, or cold, than lay out the little that is necessary to bring them so ample a return!

Each labourer represents to the state what the piece of gold is to the miser. He is the human capital of the nation and is capable of producing annual interest at the rate of at least a hundred per cent, if placed in sufficiently favourable circumstances. What folly is it then, nay what culpable negligence, nay what nothing short of criminality to sink this human gold in the bogs of beggary and destitution! Man is the most wonderful piece of machinery that exists in the world! The cleverest inventions of human science sink into insignificance in comparison with him! The whole universe is so planned that his services *cannot* be dispensed with and indeed he is at the same time the most beautiful ornament and the essential keystone of the entire fabric! The utmost that science itself can do is to increase his productive powers.

But the idea of dispensing with the service of a single human being, or of consigning him hopelessly to the perdition of beggary, destitution, famine and pestilence is the most stupendous act of folly conceivable. What should we think of a railway company that would shunt half its engines on to a siding and leave them to the destructive influence of rain and dust? And how shall we characterise the stupidity that shall shunt millions of serviceable human beings into circumstances of misery so appalling as well as of uselessness so entire, as those which we have endeavoured to picture? Why, here we have not even the decency of a siding! These wonderfully made semi-Divine human engines are suffered to obstruct the very main lines on which our expresses run, not only wrecked themselves, but the fruitful cause of wreckage to millions more!

But I have said enough I trust to show that the problem is not a hopeless one, and that the portion of General Booth's scheme to which this chapter refers is particularly applicable to India and capable of being successfully put into operation on a scale commensurate with the necessities of the hour.

Having obtained our territory we should proceed to mark it out, and to direct into the most advantageous channels, the inflowing tide of immigration. There would be a threefold division into agricultural districts which would furnish food for the incoming population, a pastoral district for the cattle, and a central market, which would furnish the pivot on which all the rest would work. Our agricultural and dairy farm proposal I have already fully discussed and will now proceed to describe the social City of Refuge which will act as a sort of solar system round which all the minor constellations would revolve.

CHAPTER XVI.
THE SOCIAL CITY OF REFUGE.

I am tempted again to turn to Hebrew history to find a parallel for what would I believe be easily accomplished at an early period in connection with our "Poor Man's Paradise." I refer to what was styled the "City of Refuge." The object of this institution was to provide a temporary shelter for those who had unintentionally killed any one, so that they might escape from "the avenger of blood." If on inquiry it could be proved that the death was purely accidental, the fugitive was entitled to claim protection until by the death of the high priest, the blood should have been expiated when he would be free to return to his home and people. If, on the other hand, it were a case of premeditated murder, the city authorities were bound to hand over the fugitive to justice.

The careful provision made by the Hebrew law for the occasional manslayer surely casts a severe reflection on the millions who, many of them through no fault of their own, represent the submerged tenth! Let us leave for the time being the wilful criminals who are the open enemies of society to be dealt with as severely as you like by the arm of the law. Turn for a moment a pitying gaze towards those hungry destitute multitudes, who cannot it may be, plead their own cause, but whose woes surely speak with an eloquence that no mere words could ever match! Why should we not provide them with a City of Refuge, where they will have a chance of regaining their feet? If it be urged that their numbers preclude such a possibility, we would reply that it has already been proved in the previous chapter, that this will in really make our task the more easy. The impetus and enthusiasm created by a movement in mass tends largely to ensure its success.

If on the other hand it be urged that our object is to divert the flow of population from cities to villages, it must be remembered that this does not preclude the creation of new towns and cities, which shall furnish convenient centres and markets for the surrounding villages. It is not a part of General Booth's scheme to abolish cities, but rather to dispose suitably of their superfluous population. And no doubt in course of time the world will be covered not only with suburban farms and industrial villages, but with cities which for commercial importance and in other respects will rival any that now exist.

I am the more encouraged to believe that this will be particularly practicable in India for the following reasons.

1. We have an enormous population close at hand. If at a distance of 12,000 to 14,000 miles, England can build its Melbournes, Sydneys and Adelaides, surely it does not require a very great stretch of imagination to suppose that here in our very midst with millions upon millions of people at disposal we shall be able to repeat what has already been elsewhere accomplished under circumstances so specially disadvantageous.

2. Again let it be remembered that in this case we should have the special advantage of carrying out the work on a carefully organised plan and in connection with a scheme possessing immense ramifications all over India and the world.

3. Once more, India supplies labor at the cheapest conceivable rate, so that the cost would be infinitesimal as compared with the other countries just mentioned.

4. Another important fact is that the laborers are accustomed to be paid in kind, and to carry on a system of exchange of goods which will further minimise the cost of the undertaking.

5. A still more encouraging element in the solving of our Indian problem is the fact that nearly every native is a skilled artizan and you can hardly meet with one who has not from childhood been taught some handicrafts. Indeed the majority both of men and women are acquainted with two or three different trades, besides being accustomed from childhood to draw their own water, wash their clothes and do their cooking. Hence it is impossible to find a more self-helpful race in the world.

6. Again this very thing has been already done in India itself, especially by its great Mahommedan rulers, hundreds of years ago, and that under circumstances, which made the undertaking infinitely more difficult than would now be the case. What was possible to them then, is equally possible to us now.

7. Finally in the midst of some of the very waste tracts of which we have spoken may be found cities which were once the flourishing centres of as large and enterprising a population as can anywhere be seen. Why should not such places be restored to their former prosperity instead of being handed over to become "the habitation of owls and dragons."

The selection of the site of the future city would of course be made with due reference to advantages of climate, water, and communication and it would be planned out previous to occupation with every consideration of convenience, health, and economy. Gangs of workmen would precede the arrival of the regular inhabitants, though we should largely rely upon the latter to build for themselves such simple yet sufficiently substantial dwellings as would meet the necessities of the case. We might reasonably anticipate, moreover, that the influx of population would attract of its own accord a certain proportion of well-to-do capitalists, for whom a special quarter of the town could be reserved and to whom special facilities could be granted for their encouragement, consistent with the general well-being of the community.

It would be easy to fill many pages with a description of the internal colony, the business routine, the simple recreations, the practical system of education for the children and the lively religious services that would constitute the daily life of the City of Refuge. Suffice it to say that we should spare no pains to promote in every way the temporal and spiritual welfare of its inhabitants, to banish drunkenness and immorality, to guard against destitution and to establish a happy holy Godfearing community, that would constitute a beacon of light and hope not only for its own immediate surroundings but far and wide for all India and the East.

CHAPTER XVII.
SUPPLEMENTARY BRANCHES OF THE COUNTRY COLONY.

(1.) *Public Works*--

While the central idea of the entire system will be that of providing permanent, as contrasted with temporary work for the destitute, there is no reason why the former should not be supplemented by the latter. The great public works which at present afford occasional relief for thousands would still be possible, only provision would be made for the redistribution of the masses of labour thus withdrawn from the ordinary channels as soon as the public work in question was completed.

For this again we possess a scriptural parallel in the "levy out of all Israel" raised by King Solomon, consisting of thirty thousand men who were sent "to Lebanon ten thousand a month by courses; a month they were in Lebanon and two months at home." In addition to the above we find that he employed seventy thousand "that bare burdens" and eighty thousand "hewers in the mountains, beside the officers which were over the work, three thousand and three hundred, which ruled over the people that wrought in the work." It was the elaborate organisation of these laborers, and the provision for their spending a certain proportion of their time at home, which enabled Solomon to carry out his great public works without seriously deranging the labor market, or hindering the prosperity of the nation. I have selected this instance because it is from well authenticated sources, goes fully into details and refers to a nation and country very much resembling India. Indeed it is almost identical with the familiar Indian institution known as "begar" or forced labour.

The weak point of such special efforts is that they tend to leave things in a worse position than ever when they are concluded. Nobody sits down to calculate what is to become of the thousands who have been drawn together, often hundreds of miles from their homes, when the time comes for them to be paid off. They are thrown bodily upon the labor market and left to shift for themselves as best they can, without any means of informing themselves where they ought to go, or into what other channels they can most profitably direct their labor.

This evil we hope to obviate by means of our Labor Bureaux, which will be planted in every city and district, and will keep such elaborate returns as will enable to watch all the fluctuations of the labor market.

For instance let us be informed of the fact that a railway is to be opened, a canal dug, or some other public work constructed in a particular district, we should be able to calculate from our returns the amount of labor that could conveniently be withdrawn from existing channels, and the amount that would have to be imported.

We should be able to constitute a Solomon's levy (voluntary of course), and the laborers would have the assurance that when the work on which they were engaged was concluded, sufficient provision would be made for their reemployment elsewhere, or for their restoration to their ordinary occupation. Our Labor Bureau would thus do for the laborer what is at present impossible for him to do for himself, and would economise his time to the utmost.

(2.) *Off to the Tea Gardens*--

We should be able again to supply the Tea and Coffee Districts with gangs of laborers, and should guard the interests of both employer and employed. The former would be supplied with picked laborers at the ordinary market rate, without the worry, delay and expense of having to procure them for themselves. The latter would be kept in communication with their families, and could be worked in "courses" on Solomon's plan.

(3.) *Land along the Railways*--

Among other proposals General Booth suggests that the land along the Railway lines might well be utilised for the purpose of spade husbandry. There seems no reason why these extensive strips of often fertile soil should be left to go to waste, conveniently situated as they are on borders of the main arteries of commerce and in close vicinity to stations.

(4.) *Improved methods of Agriculture*--

This is a subject which deserves a chapter to itself in a country like India. If it be true that there are millions of acres of waste land that are only waiting to be cultivated to yield a rich return, it is equally notorious that by improved methods of agriculture the present produce of the soil may be doubled and trebled. To this subject we intend to pay the full attention that it deserves, making the best possible use of Native experience and European science. We shall be in a peculiarly favorable situation for experiments on a large scale. But this is a subject on which we cannot at present do more than touch, reserving for a future period the elaboration of schemes which will doubtless have an enormous reflexive effect upon the whole of India, and thus materially increase the wealth of the entire country and the revenue of the Government.

CHAPTER XVIII.
THE OVER-SEA COLONY.

As in England, so in India, the establishment of a colony over the sea will in the end prove the necessary completion of our scheme for supplying work to the workless. There are sure to be found eventually in over-crowded centres many for whom work at home cannot be found, and for whom vast reaches of unoccupied territories in other lands wait to afford a home.

Happily this will not be an immediate necessity in India. Over the extended area occupied by the various races which comprise the Indian Empire, large tracts of land still wait to be conquered by well-directed industry, and the numerous settlements which it will be possible to form in different parts of the country may for some time to come absorb the surplus labour, add to the wealth of the country, the stability of the Empire and the more rapid advancement of the Kingdom of Christ. Since, however, we must look forward to emigration as the ultimate solution of the problem which confronts us, we shall briefly indicate the lines upon which we propose to carry it out.

In the establishment of Over-sea Colonies we shall follow very closely the lines laid down in "Darkest England."

At present the continuous stream of emigrant labour flowing into existing colonies already overstocked with labor, is creating serious difficulties, and we have no idea of relieving a congested labour market in one country by overstocking another: this would be, not to heal the disorder, but only to shift the locality.

It may not be generally known how extensively emigration is already resorted to by the people of India. We know that the impression is abroad that Indians will not leave their country, that they fear the sea, are too much attached to their home and their customs, and are far too much filled with the dread of losing caste to yield to any pressure that may be brought to bear upon them to quit the shores of their own land for foreign fields of labour. As a matter of fact, however, emigration to a considerable extent already exists.

In Ceylon alone there are nearly 300,000 Tamil coolies employed on the Tea Estates, besides hundreds of thousands more who have permanently settled in various parts of the Island. Vast tracts in the Island are still waiting to be occupied. The former population of Ceylon is variously estimated as having been from twelve to thirty millions,--now it is only three! Is it impossible for us to suppose that it can be restored to its former prosperity? Immense tanks and irrigation works cover the entire country in tracts which are now unoccupied and desolate. Many of these have been restored by Government, and there are now 100,000 acres of irrigable land in that country, only waiting to be occupied and cultivated. Government is ready to give it on easy terms. Here, then, alone is a wide and hopeful field for Indian emigration, only requiring to be skilfully directed in order to find a home and living for millions of India's destitute.

Now what we propose to do is not to check the stream of emigration, nor yet to help it to flow on in its present channel until it overflows its banks and engulfs in ruin the colonies it might have enriched, but rather to dig out new channels, founding entirely new colonies in districts yet unoccupied, on the plan laid down in "Darkest England."

The stream which, diverted into 20 or 30 channels, would enrich and fertilize a whole continent, would if confined to one or two channels burst its banks and become a desolating flood.

We shall ourselves become the leaders of the coolies, and dig out channels in Ceylon, in Africa, in South America, and other countries, building up from entirely new centres new colonies and territories and kingdoms where the Indian colonist would find himself not a stranger in a strange land, unwelcome, neglected, or ill-treated, but at home in a new India, more prosperous and happy than the one he had left behind,--a colony peopled and possessed and managed by those of his own race and language.

Emigration carried on simply in the interests of those who promote it and derive a profit out of it, without regard to the needs of the districts to which they are exported, and with absolute disregard to the comfort and convenience of the emigrant, and often attended with heartless cruelties, must necessarily be fraught with grave evils. These we believe we should largely be able to obviate. In vessels chartered by ourselves or in some way under our direction, and with every comfort and convenience which can be secured for the limited sum available for cost of transit, for men, women, and children, under the direct superintendence of our own trained officers, what a curtailment of human suffering and shame there will be in the transit of the Colonist alone! On his arrival he will be met by those who, if strangers, are his friends, and who will secure for him comfortable quarters, communicate, or enable the emigrant to communicate, with his friends at home, introduce him to the particular industry to which he is assigned, and who will not cease their personal care of him until he is happily settled in his new home, and who will afterwards be available for advice and counsel. He will find himself, not amongst people who are eager to secure their own profit at his expense, but a part of a commonwealth where each is taught to seek the good of his neighbour, and where the laws are framed to secure and perpetuate this desirable condition of things. A community where the blessings of home and education and sanitary laws and religion are valued and made available for all, and where liberty, which nowhere shines so sweetly as amongst a frugal, industrious, intelligent, simple and godly people, reigns in truth.

Moreover, our widely extended operations, our connection and oneness with the great social movement of the Army in various lands, and the regulations which will control the movement, will enable us invariably to convey our colonists to fields where their labours will be of the greatest value, and instantly to check any tendency to excess of labour at any given centre, and even at times to greatly relieve temporary gluts in the labor market arising from unforeseen circumstances.

In short, it is scarcely possible to overrate the blessings likely to flow from Colonies where drink and opium will be unprocurable, where vice will be repressed, where greed will receive little encouragement and have few opportunities to grow, and where the comparative absence of poverty on the one hand, and of extreme wealth on the other and the general contentment of the people, will make life on earth a joy to those who were once nearly starved out of it.

CHAPTER XIX.
MISCELLANEOUS AGENCIES.

(1) THE INTELLIGENCE DEPARTMENT.

In connection with our Labor Bureau we shall establish an intelligence department, the duty of which will be to collect all kinds of information likely to be of use in prosecuting our Social Reform.

For instance, it would watch the state of the labor market, would ascertain where there was a lack of labor and where a glut, would inform the public of the progress of the movement, would bring to our notice any newspaper criticisms or suggestions, and would generally make itself useful in a thousand ways.

(2) THE POOR MAN'S LAWYER.

This would meet a long-felt want, and could also be worked in connection with the Labor Bureau.

The poor would be able to get sound legal advice in regard to their difficulties, and we should be able to help them in their defence where we believed them to be wronged.

(3) THE INQUIRY OFFICE FOR MISSING FRIENDS.

This has been established for some time in England with admirable success, our worldwide organization enabling us to trace people under the most unfavorable circumstances. No doubt there would be much scope for such a department in India. At the outset it would form part of the duties of the Labor Bureau, and would not therefore entail any extra expense.

(4) THE MATRIMONIAL BUREAU.

A thoroughly confidential matrimonial bureau which would wisely advise people desirous of getting married, would certainly be of great service in India. Its operations would no doubt be small in the beginning, but as it got to be known and trusted it would be more and more resorted to.

Even supposing that outsiders should hold aloof from it, we should have a large inside constituency to whom its operations would be very valuable, and it would be thoroughly in accordance with native notions for the mutual negotiations to be carried on in such a way.

Missionaries are everywhere largely resorted to in regard to questions of this kind; and we have every reason to believe that it would be so with ourselves, and we should thus be able largely to guard our people against ill-assorted matches, and to furnish them with wise counsel on the subject.

(5) THE EMIGRATION BUREAU.

The subject of emigration has been already referred to elsewhere. No doubt we shall ultimately require a separate and special office for this purpose in all the chief cities but at the outset its duties would fall upon the Labor Bureau and Intelligence Departments who would collect all the information they could preparatory to the launching of this part of the scheme.

(6) PERIODICAL MELAS.

In place of the "Whitechapel by the sea" proposed by General Booth, a suitable Indian substitute would I think consist of periodical "melas" similar to those already prevalent in various parts of the country.

These might be arranged with the treble object of religious instruction, bodily recreation, and in order to find an occasional special market for the surplus goods that we produce.

Everything would be managed with military precision. The place would be previously prepared for the reception of the people. An attractive programme would be arranged. Everybody would be made to feel comfortable and at home. And no effort would be spared to make the occasion morally and spiritually profitable, as well as valuable for the relaxation it afforded to the bodies of those who attended, and financially profitable for the purpose of our Social Reform work.

CHAPTER XX.
HOW MUCH WILL IT COST?

In order to put the whole of the foregoing machinery into motion on an extensive scale, there can be no doubt that economise as we may, a considerable outlay will be unavoidable. True we are able to supply skilled leadership under devoted and self-sacrificing men and women for a merely nominal cost. True we have Europeans willing to live on the cheap native diet, and to assimilate themselves in dress, houses and other manners to the people amongst whom they live. True that we have raised up around us an equally devoted band of Natives, in whose integrity we have the fullest confidence and whose ability and knowledge of the country will prove of valuable service to us in the carrying out of our scheme. True that around our 450 European and Native officers, we have enlisted and drilled a force of several thousands of earnest soldiers of the Cross, who are pledged abstainers from all intoxicating liquors and drugs, who have renounced all forms of impurity and sin,--who have promised to devote their lives to the social, moral and spiritual regeneration of their fellow countrymen,--who are accustomed to pray and preach in their leisure hours, without being paid a cowrie for doing so, and who not only support themselves and their families by their labor, but contribute for the support of their officers.

Nevertheless, while it is a fact that this cheap and efficient agency exists for the carrying out of the reforms that have been sketched in the foregoing pages,--it cannot be denied that a considerable sum of money will be needed for the successful launching of the scheme.

Once fairly started, we have every reason to believe that the plans here laid down will not only prove strictly self-supporting, but will yield such a margin of profit as will ultimately enable us to set on foot wholesale extensions of the scheme.

No doubt there will be local disappointments and individual failures. We are deal-ing with human nature, and must anticipate that this will be the case. But the pro-portion of success will far outweigh the fraction of failure, and when the profits and losses of the scheme came to be balanced year by year we have no doubt that socially, physically, morally and financially we shall be able to show so enormous a gain that the most unreasonable of our critics will be silenced.

And yet when we come face to face with the details of the scheme, we find that the scale of our operations must necessarily depend on the amount of capital with which we are able to start. The City Colony, with its Labor Bureau, Labor Yards, Food Depots, Prison and Rescue Homes, and Salvage Brigade, will involve a consid-erable initial expense. Although we are able to supply an efficient supervising staff for a mere fraction of the ordinary cost,--rents of land and buildings will have to paid. And although work will be exacted from those who resort to our Yards and Homes, yet the supply of food to the large numbers who are likely to need our help will at the outset probably cost us more than we are able to recover from the sale of the goods produced.

The Country Colony, with its Industrial Villages, Suburban Farms, and Waste Settlements, will involve a still heavier outlay of capital. There is every reason to believe that we may look for an ample return. Indeed the financial prospects of this branch of the scheme are more hopeful than these of the City Colony. But to commence on a large scale will involve no doubt a proportionate expenditure. We may hope indeed that Government, Native States and private landowners will gen-erously assist us to overcome these difficulties by grants of land, and advances of money and other concessions. Still we must anticipate that a considerable portion of the financial burden and responsibility in commencing such an enterprise must of necessity fall upon us.

The Over-Sea Colony may for the present be postponed, and hence we have not now to consider what would be the probable expenses. But omitting this, and having regard only to the City and Country Colonies, I believe that to make a com-mencement on a fairly extensive scale we shall require a sum of one lakh of rupees. We do not pretend that with this sum at our command we can do more than make a beginning. It would be idle to suppose that the miseries of twenty-five millions of people could be annihilated at a stroke for such a sum.

We do believe however that by sinking such a sum we should be able to manufacture a road over which a continuous and increasing mass of the Submerged would be able to liberate themselves from their present miserable surroundings and rise to a position of comparative comfort.

We are confident moreover that the profits, or shall we call them the tolls paid by those who passed over this highway, would enable us speedily to construct a second, which would be broader and better than the first. The first two would multiply themselves to four, the four to eight, the eight to sixteen, till the number and breadth of these social highways would be such as to place deliverance within easy reach of all who desired it.

The sum we ask for is less than a tithe of what has been so speedily raised in England for the rescue of a far smaller number of the submerged. And yet there may be those who will think that we are asking for too much. But when I see far larger sums expended on the erection, or support of a single Hospital, or Dharamsala, and when I remember that Indian philanthropy has covered the country with such, I am tempted to exclaim "What is this among so many?"

Surely it would be a libel upon Indian philanthropy and generosity to ask for less, in launching a scheme, which has received the hearty support of multitudes of persons so well able to form a judgment as to its feasibility and soundness, and this too after having been submitted to the most searching criticisms that human ingenuity could suggest! At any rate this we can promise, that whatever may be given will be laid out carefully to the best possible advantage. A special annual balance sheet will show how the money entrusted to our care has been expended, and if the success of the work be not sufficient to justify its existence, it will always be easy for the public to withhold those supplies on which we must continue to depend for the prosecution of our enterprise.

Looking at the future however in the light of the past history of the Salvation Army, both in India, and especially in those other parts of the world, where its organization has had more time to develop and fewer obstacles to contend with, we are confident that the results will be such as to repay a hundred fold every effort made and every rupee laid out in promoting the welfare of India. And even supposing that comparative failure should result, we should have the satisfaction of knowing that

"'Tis better to have tried and failed,   Than never to have tried at all!"

The anathemas of posterity will alight upon the heads, not of those who have made a brave effort to better the evils that surround them, but of those who by their supineness helped to ensure such failure, or by their active opposition paralysed the efforts and discouraged the hearts of those who, but for them, might either have wholly succeeded in accomplishing what all admit to be so desirable, or might at least have been far nearer reaching their goal than was possible owing to the dog-in-the-manger obstructions of those who had neither the heart to help, nor the brains to devise, nor the courage to execute, what others might have dared and done!

CHAPTER XXI.
A PRACTICAL CONCLUSION.

In proposing at once to deal with the problem of lifting out of the jaws of starvation India's poorest and darkest however impossible it may look to some, we have the immense advantage and encouragement which arises from the fact that General Booth's scheme (which I have followed as closely as the widely differing conditions of Indian society would admit) has already received the all but universal approval of the best and ablest in Europe from the Queen downwards. It has in fact so commended itself to the general public that men of all shades of religious belief, men of no belief at all, men of every political party, and from every rank of society have not only heartily approved but contributed already L100,000 for the carrying out of the project. Moreover, some of its most important details have already had applied to them both in England and Australia the valuable test of experience.

There is one question which may start up in the mind of the reader and that is, granted that the scheme is sure to prove successful in England, is it not still probable that, owing to the complex arrangements of caste and religion in India any such scheme would meet with failure. To this I answer in the first place, that all will be helped, irrespective of their creed, and any change of opinions on their part will be purely voluntary, since no compulsion, beyond that of love and moral suasion, is intended to be used. Moreover, drowning men are not too particular as to the means available for their rescue. They would rather be dragged out of the water by the hair of their heads than left to drown, or would rather be lifted out feet foremost than left to be devoured by alligators. If it be true that starving men are driven by hunger to commit theft solely that they may be sent to jail where at least they will get food and be saved for a time from the hunger-wolf, how can we doubt but that thousands will hail with gladness a deliverance which is not only a deliverance from want and starvation, but the opening out of a brighter path for their whole future.

The blessed example set by hundreds of men and women in our ranks who have given up friends, parents, home, prospects and everything they possess to walk barefooted beneath India's burning sun in order to seek the weal of its people cannot fail I believe to stir up the rich and well-to-do, nay *all* but those too poor to help,--to make some sacrifice to heal the unutterable woes, and to sweeten the hard and bitter lot of those who, often through no fault of their own, have fallen in the battle of life, and who have been all but crushed and cursed out of existence by misfortunes which are to some extent at least within our power to remedy.

True lovers of India (and nothing is more encouraging than the splendid manner in which the intelligence of this country is arousing itself to thoughtful active effort for the weal of the nation, putting aside all differences of race and religion, that it may unite to seek the common good,) true lovers of India, we say, will never allow differences in race and religion to hinder them in a question affecting the well-being of some 26,000,000 of people who are already a drag and a hindrance to the rising prosperity of the nation, and who are sure if neglected to become a danger. No one asks about the religion of Stanley. His heroic march through the terrible forest, his rescue of Emin Pasha, his successful achievement of that which to most men would have been impossible, have made him to be admired and praised in every land.

Here we are proposing to rescue, not one Pasha and a handful of his followers, but almost as many people as the entire population of Great Britain. We stand at the edge of this forest. We know something of it before we enter. We are not dismayed. We only ask you to meet the cost of the expedition. Great armies of beggars and workless, and drunkards and opium-eaters and harlots and criminals are going to be dragged out of these morasses, to bless the land which gave them birth with the wealth of their labor and to build new Indian Empires across the sea.

A bold and daring expedition has been planned into this dark social forest, with its dismal swamps, its pestilential vapours, its seemingly endless night, to rescue and bring to the light of hope, to green industrial pastures and healthy heavenly breezes, its imprisoned victims. May we not then, since men can be found to do and dare in such a godlike enterprise, confidently claim the enthusiastic interest and the practical help of all good men, no matter when or how they worship the great Eternal Father of the human race!

If any one should object that is an impossible enterprise, we answer, who can tell? Why indeed impossible, seeing that millions of acres wait to be tilled and to yield their treasures to the unfed mouths of workless labourers? Why impossible, since hundreds of thousands are saying, it is not charity, we crave, but the privilege to work and earn our bread? Why impossible, when willing hearts and hands are ready to spring forward and at any cost dive into this dark forest and bring the hungry mouths into the fostering care of the fruitful earth? Why impossible, when a mass of unproductive wealth waits to serve some useful purpose and bless its holder, bringing back to him a hundred per cent, if he will but lend it to his God by giving it to the poor?

We have portrayed with studied moderation the dark regions of woe. We have laid before you with careful explicitness the scheme or remedy. We have endeavoured to anticipate and answer all objections. And now it is for you to make this great enterprise possible by uniting to subscribe the sum we ask for, as necessary to float the scheme.

We have built our deliverance ship in the dockyard of loving design, we have wrought her plates, riveted her bolts, fixed her masts, put in her boilers and engines, fitted her and supplied her with gear. It is your privilege to launch her--to draw the silver bolt and permit her to leave the stocks and glide down into the dark deep sea of misery and land on heavenly shores the drowning submerged millions.

We believe that your response will be worthy of you. Coming generations will thank you, and the blessings of them that were ready to perish will rest upon you, and the God of the fatherless and the widow will remember you for good.

APPENDIX.

The Poor Whites and Eurasians.

It will doubtless be noticed that I have excluded the consideration of this question from the foregoing pages. This has been decided on, though with considerable hesitation, for the following reasons:--

1. Numerically they are much fewer than the submerged India of which we have been speaking.

2. Influential charitable agencies already exist, whose special duty it is to care for them; any effort on our part to apply General Booth's scheme to them would probably be regarded by those societies as a work of supererogation, and would be likely to be received by them with a considerable measure of opposition.

3. The circumstances and surroundings of the European and Eurasian community are so different that the scheme will require considerable readaptation. Indeed the subject will need a pamphlet to itself, and I have found it impossible to work it harmoniously into the present scheme.

4. I am convinced moreover that this is a *subsidiary* question, and that our main efforts *must* be directed towards reaching and uplifting the purely Indian submerged.

5. Should however the question be pressed upon us hereafter, we shall be quite prepared to take it up and deal with it systematically and radically on the lines laid down by General Booth. I have studied with considerable care and interest the writings of the late Mr. White on this important matter, and believe that if the necessary funds were forthcoming, it would be comparatively easy for us to adapt the Darkest England Scheme to the necessities of this important class.

PUBLIC OPINION ON GENERAL BOOTH'S SOCIAL SCHEME.

Her Majesty the Queen-Empress cordially sympathises.

Her Majesty says "The Queen cannot of course express any opinion on the details of the scheme, but understanding that your object is to alleviate misery and suffering, her Majesty cordially wishes you success in the undertaking you have originated."

His Royal Highness, The Prince of Wales,

Writes to express his hearty interest in the scheme and is seen earnestly studying the book and making notes upon it.

The Empress Frederick reads the book with interest.

THE EMPRESS FREDERICK'S PALACE, BERLIN,

November 1, 1890.

Count Seckendorff begs leave to acknowledge by command of her Majesty the Empress Frederick the receipt of General Booth's book in "Darkest England and the way out." Count Seckendorff is commanded to say that her Majesty will read the book with special interest.

The Earl of Aberdeen expresses his sympathy.

In common with thousands of others I have been studying your "plan of campaign." Last night I saw Mr. Bancroft's letter. I think he has performed a public service in coming forward in this spirited manner at the present time. Those who have been in any way associated with past or existing efforts on behalf of the classes which you aim at reaching should reasonably be amongst the first to welcome a scheme so practical, so comprehensive, and so carefully devised as that which you have placed before the country. I shall be happy to become one of the hundred contributors who according to Mr. Bancroft's proposal shall each be responsible for L1,000 on the condition specified. With the offer of sympathy, and the assurance of hearty good wishes,

I remain, yours very faithfully,

ABERDEEN.

The Earl of Airlie Subscribes.

"The Earl of Airlie has forwarded towards General Booth's fund a cheque for L1,000."

The Marquis of Queensberry offers his services.

GLENLEE, NEW GALLOWAY, N.B.,

November 21.

My Dear General Booth--I have read your book "In Darkest England" with the greatest interest, also with thrills of horror that things should be as bad as they are.

I send you a cheque for L100, and shall feel compelled if your scheme is carried out to give you a yearly subscription. You say you want recruits. When I come to town I should very much like to see you to talk this matter over, for I see no cause which a man could more put his heart and soul into than this one of endeavouring to alleviate this fearful misery of our fellow-creatures. I see you quote Carlyle in your book, but is it possible for any one like myself, who is even more bitterly opposed than he was against what to me is the Christian falsehood, to work with you! We have two things to do as things are at present--first to endeavour to alleviate the present awful suffering that exists to the best of our abilities, and surely this ought to be a state affair; and secondly to get at the roots of the evils and by changing public opinion gradually develop a different state of things for future generations, when this help will not be so necessary. I do not wish to get into a religious controversy with you on how this is to be brought about, but I tell you I am no Christian and am bitterly opposed to it. A tree, I believe, is to be judged by its fruits. Christianity has been with us many hundreds of years.

What can we think of it when its results are as they are at present with the poor whom Christ, I believe, you say informed us we should always have with us. I know nothing about other worlds, beyond that I see thousand around me whom I presume look after their own affairs. It appears to me our common and plainest duty to help and to try and change the lot of our suffering fellow creatures here on this earth. You can publish this if you please, but without suppressing any of it. If not and any notice is given of subscriptions as I see you are doing, I beg it may be notified that I send this mite as a reverent agnostic to our common cause of humanity.

Yours faithfully,

QUEENSBERRY.

Lord Scarborough is amongst its supporters.

"Lord Scarborough, writing from Lumley Castle Chester-le-street, has subscribed L50."

Mr. and Mrs. Gladstone lend to it the weight of their influence.

"Mr. Gladstone has already expressed has interest in the scheme and now Mr.

and Mrs. Gladstone with a like kindly expression forward L50 towards it."

Mr. Pickersgill, M.P., looks upon it with increasing favour.

At the New Debating Society, Haverstook Hill, Mr. Pickersgill, M.P., said when he first began to read the book he did not approach it with any particularly favourable feelings towards the Salvation Army. He thought that the scheme was the most plausible ever devised. There was in it a happy blending of the ideal with the practical, and a nice balancing of its various parts in the attempt to solve the problem involved in the question "Can we get back to the ordinary conditions of life as they exist in a small healthy community."

The Bishop of Durham reviews the Scheme.

Speaking on Thursday night at the closing meeting of the General Church Mission at Sunderland, the Bishop of Durham said that just now men were talking on all sides of a great scheme which had been set forth for dealing with some of the social sorrows of our age. The remarkable book in which it was sketched was well calculated to present, in a most vivid combination, the various forms of work to which Christian men must bring the power of their faith. It brought together with remarkable skill the different problems which were pressed upon them; it allowed them to gain a view of the whole field and something of the relation of the different parts one to another. For his own part he trusted that many might be stirred to some unwonted exertion.

The Bishop of Lincoln thanks the General.

"I thank you heartily for the book you have sent me. The name of it is already well known to English Churchmen, and its object is one in which, we all agree.

"The Cross of Christ is the only effectual remedy for the great mass of vice and wretchedness in our large towns, to which you are endeavouring to call public attention; and we must not be content with presenting that Cross in words alone, but must endeavour to show, by our personal efforts and example, how it may practically be applied so as to purify the lives and quicken the hopes of those amongst our countrymen who are now as much strangers to its power as the inhabitants of darkest Africa."

The Bishop of Bath and Wells values the book.

"I beg to acknowledge, with very many thanks, the receipt of your letter and the volume of your work, 'In Darkest England,' which you have been so good as to send me. I shall read it with much interest, both from the deep importance of the subject, whether viewed in its social, political, or Christian aspect, and also from its containing the opinion of one who has had such universal opportunities as you have had of becoming acquainted with the wants of the lowest and most unhappy section of our great population."

The Bishop of Rochester is glad to possess the book.

The Bishop of Rochester writes that he hastens to thank Mr. Booth for sending him his book, and he is glad to possess it, and hopes it may be productive of much good. He takes the opportunity of expressing his profound sympathy with him in Mrs. Booth's death.

The Bishop of Wakefield (Dr. Walsham How) studies the scheme with deepest interest.

I have just received your book, which you have so kindly sent me. I have already bought a copy, which I shall give away. I am studying your scheme with the deepest interest, and I trust and pray it may bring blessing and hope to many. May I venture to express my sympathy with you in your recent heavy bereavement? You do not sorrow as those that have no hope.

Canon Farrar preaching at Westminster Abbey, says we are bound to help the scheme or find a better one.

It was not difficult to see, as early as half past one on Sunday afternoon last, that something was about to take place in Westminister Abbey. A friendly policeman informed me that the service in the fine old pile of buildings did not commence till three o'clock, but that as Canon Farrar was announced to preach, and upon such an all-absorbing topic as General Booth's new book, people were bent upon securing a good position by being in time.

Some three-quarters of an hour before the service commenced the gigantic building was crowded, and the trooping multitudes only arrived at the doors to find a crowd waiting for the least opportunity of getting in. It was reported that thousands were turned away.

Canon Farrar had announced his subject as "Social Amelioration," and at the outset stated that he alone was responsible for the opinions he proposed to express in connection with General Booth's scheme. In a very masterly and eloquent way he pictured the social evils which disgrace our civilisation, the small and ineffectual efforts being put forth for their removal, and the terrible responsibility resting upon us as a nation to do our utmost to forward any scheme which appeared likely to effect an amelioration. He proceeded:--

Well, here was General Booth's scheme, which he had examined, and with which he had been deeply struck. He pitied the cold heart which could read and not be stirred by "Darkest England." In his best judgment he believed the scheme to be full of promise if the necessary funds were provided, and he merely regarded it as his humble duty to render the undertaking such aid as he could.

Had any such scheme been proposed by a member of the Church of England, he should have given it every support. He regarded the scheme as supplementing, not interfering with, the work of the Church, as preparing for, not hindering, the Church's work. The scheme, although no Christian scheme could be wholly dis-linked from religion, was yet most prominently a social scheme; its origin was The Salvation Army, but it was intended to promote the work of the common Church.

Was the scheme to be thrown aside contemptuously at once on account of prejudice, because it emanated from The Salvation Army? If any thought so, he blamed them not, but he for one declared he could not share their views. He was, perhaps, more widely separated from some of the methods of the Salvation Army than many of his brethren, but the work of the Army had not been unblessed, and there was much that might be learned from an organisation which in so short a time had accomplished so great a work. He dwelt upon the nature of The Salvation Army's work, the officers who were exerting themselves in connection with it, the number of countries to which the organisation had spread. The Salvation Army in its work and extent had credentials which could not be denied. Were they to stand coldly, finically aside because they were too refined and nice, and full of culture to touch this work of The Salvation Army with the point of the finger? He took it that he should fail grievously in his duty if insult or self-interest caused him to hold aloof from any movement which Christ, if He had been on earth, would have approved.

Then Dr. Farrar quoted the late Bishop Lightfoot and the late Canon Liddon in favor of The Salvation Army as an organisation which had accomplished a deal of good work.

Next he asked, "How shall we receive General Booth's scheme now that it is here to our hands?" With some people the simplest way of treating any scheme for good was to leave it alone. To those who took that position with reference to General Booth's scheme he had nothing whatever to say. There was no need for saying anything either to the other class of people who would talk about a scheme, and having talked about it drop the matter and think no more about it.

Another way in which General Booth's scheme might be received was that of examining it, and if convinced against it of rejecting it. That, at all events, was a perfectly manly course; a clear and decided method of reception which there can be no mistaking. To those included in this class, those who would regard the scheme as migratory or pernicious, there was nothing to be said. But what about those who did not mean to help in this or any other scheme, those who left others the burden of the work, the opportunists who would want to step in when the breach had been made? Here, no doubt, there would be such a class, but the last way of receiving General Booth's scheme, and the way in which as he trusted it would be received, was to support it by their influence, and to give to it of their means. It was an immense and far-reaching scheme, which, might bring help and hope to thousands of the helpless and hopeless, made helpless and hopeless by the terrible conditions of society, but for every one of whom Christ died.

To begin the scheme in earnest would require a sum of L100,000, but he asked, "What was that to the wealth of England--to the wealth of London?" It was a mere drop in the ocean compared to what was every year spent on drink and wasted in extravagance. There were a hundred men in England who might immortalise themselves by giving this sum, and yet not have a luxury the less. He left the response to General Booth's appeal with the public, but would it not, he asked, be a desperate shame for England if any scheme giving so hopeful a promise of social amelioration should fail without a trial, and like a broken promise, be lost in air?

But to this observation somebody might reply in the form of a queried objection, "The scheme might fail." *Yes, it might fail; anything might fail. But if to die amid disloyalty and hatred meant failure, then St. Paul failed. If to die in the storm meant failure, then Luther and Wesley and Whitfield failed; if to die at the stake by the flames meant failure, did not martyrs fail; Finally, if to die on the cross, with the priests and the soldiers spitting out hatred, meant failure, then Jesus Christ failed.* Yes, the scheme might fail; but was all this failure? Were there none among them bold enough to look beyond the possibility of failure? Could they not somehow get round the word? Fear and jealousy and suspicion and intolerance and despair were counsellors finding multitudes to listen, but he for one would listen to the nobler counsellor "Hope." Were none of them bold enough at the last moment to prefer even failure in a matter like this to the most brilliant success in pleasing the world and making truce with the devil? He would try to hope that the scheme might not fail, but what each one had to consider was the question, "Shall it fail through my cowardice, my greed, my supineness, my prudential cautiousness, my petty prejudices, my selfish conventionality?"

"If, on examining this plan in the light of conscience, we see in it an augury for the removal of the deadly evils which lie at the heart of our civilisation, it seems to me we are bound to do our utmost to help it forward. 'But,' you say, 'if we conscientiously disapprove of it?' Then we are in duty bound to propose or to forward SOMETHING BETTER.

"One way only is contemptible and accursed--that is, to make it a mere excuse for envy, malice and depreciation.

"He that heareth, let him hear; and he that forbeareth, let him forbear; but God shall be the judge between us, and His voice says in Scripture: 'If thou forbear to deliver them that are bound unto death, and those who are ready to be slain; if thou sayest, "Behold," we knew it not, doth not He that pondereth the heart consider it, and he that keepeth thy soul, doth not He know it, and shall not He render to every man according to his work?'"

Archdeacon Sinclair wishes the scheme success.

Speaking at Bromley, Kent, on Friday night, in connection with the Canterbury diocese, of the Church of England Temperance Society, Archdeacon Sinclair referred to General Booth's scheme. He wished very great success to that courageous and large scheme.

The Rev. Brooke Lambert defends the scheme in the "Times."

There is much that is not new in the scheme. General Booth allows that much. But there are two factors in his scheme which, if not new, at least acquire a new prominence. These two factors are help and hope. Society drops these two h's. For help it substitutes money-giving, and as for hope for the disreputable, it has none. The personal contact of General Booth's workers, of his 10,000 officers, is an essential feature of the scheme. They take the man or the woman as they enter the shelter, and prevent it from becoming a means of dissemination of crime, of filth, of disease. They stand by the new-fledged proselyte to work, to encourage perseverance. They follow him to the country colony, the abomination of desolation to one who has walked the London pavements and found his heaven in the gin-palace and the music-hall, to stimulate effort. They accompany him to the colony to remind him that true freedom is not licence, that the conditions of success are a change of mind and not of climate. But for them, one might doubt whether the hope General Booth conceives for the "submerged tenth" would be hope at all in their eyes. Nothing so difficult as to persuade the Londoner to go into the country, and the emigrant to keep to work away from the congenial interludes of town pleasure. But once create this hope (and persistent reiteration can do much when the agent is a kindly man or woman) and you have introduced a new element into the life of the wastrel. Our prison system, growing in harshness, failed utterly to deter; with the reformatory system, based on the principle of making it to a man's interest to behave well within the walls, a new era dawned on criminal legislation. It is for these reasons that I look with deep interest on General Booth's experiment. Do not let us say, "The experiment has been tried before; it is useless to attempt it again." I believe there is enough of novelty in General Booth's scheme to justify a hope of success. But for past failures I can but say that people do not regard failure as a ground for inaction when their interest is deeply involved. When I was a boy, some 45 years ago, I saw at the old Polytechnic experiments in electricity: the electric light, the electric cautery, &c. For years I expected to see them introduced into the work-day world. Now, at last, they are coming into use, but I do not think the shares stand at a very high premium. None the less electricity will one day be of universal use. That is what experiment in spite of failure has done; that is what we ought to do in social matters. When all is done, the result will be comparatively small when compared with our aspirations, but it will create, as all good work does, new outlets for effort, new objects for hope.

BROOKE LAMBERT.

The Vicarage, Greenwich, Nov. 19.

Dr. Parker approves the General's Scheme.

A report in the *Star* says:--"Dr. Parker, preaching his one-minute sermon at the City Temple yesterday (Sunday) morning, said, 'I hope General Booth will get every penny he asked for. No man can make better use of money. I wish be would include other Englands in his scheme. There is another England, darker than the darkest he has in view. I mean the England of genteel poverty and genteel misery.... These people are not in the slums, but they are fast being driven in that direction.... From my point of view, one of the best features in General Booth's scheme is that nobody is to receive anything for nothing. It is easy to throw money away. Money we work for goes farthest. There is

NO STAIN OF PAUPERISM

upon it.

DR. PARKER SAYS "NO BOARDS."--Dr. Parker, addressing his congregation on Thursday morning, said:--"General Booth spoke to me the other day at my house, amongst others, about boards of trustees and referees, and all the rest of it, in reference to his scheme. I said that would spoil the whole thing. I do not want any boards of reference. We have boards enough and referees enough--(laughter)-- and we do not want little men to assume an awful responsibility which Providence never meant them to handle. They had better let a great governing spirit like General Booth manage the whole thing in his own way. I am afraid I was even more of a democrat than even General Booth suspected. (Laughter.) I am an autocrat--I believe in one man doing a thing. Some persons imagine if they have got six little men together that they will total up into a Booth. The Lord makes His own Booths, and Moodys, and Spurgeons, and sends them out to do His work, and we shall do well to get out of their way, except when we have anything to give of sympathy, money, prayer and assistance. Presently, some Thursday morning, I am going to give you a chance of giving--which you will--to this great scheme." (Applause.)

Dr. Moulton, President of the Wesleyan Conference, is grateful for the labour which the General has expended upon this problem.

"No one can read your book without recognising the claim which you have established on the sympathetic help of all Christian churches. For myself, I am deeply grateful to you for the enormous labor which you have expended on the great problem, and for your able treatment of its difficulties."

Revd. Alfred Rowland says he believes the working of the Scheme will be for the good of the people.

Yesterday morning the Rev. Alfred Rowland preached at Park Chapel, Crouch

End, the first portion of a sermon on General Booth's book. The preacher said the scheme was a noble, bold, and generous effort to reach the masses. He believed the result of the working of the scheme would be for the good of the people at large. He asked them to give liberally to the project, even if it was only an experiment, because he believed it would succeed, and all he could do, financially and otherwise, he should be pleased to do in support of the scheme.

A Collection for the Scheme is raised at City Church, Oxford.

At the City Church, Oxford, on Sunday, the rector, the Rev. Carterel J.H. Fletcher, preached at both morning and evening services in aid of General Booth's Social Salvation Fund, and the collections were devoted to the object.

Revd. H. Arnold Thomas makes a successful appeal on behalf of the Scheme.

A HANDSOME OFFERING.

The sum of L650 was collected at Highbury Congregational Chapel, Bristol, on Sunday, as a contribution to General Booth's fund, for his scheme unfolded in his book, "In Darkest England." This was in response to an appeal from the pastor, the Rev. H. Arnold Thomas.

Revd. Champness looks upon it as a forlorn hope.

A letter dated from Rochdale, and bearing the well-known name "Thomas Champness," has reached General Booth, with a contribution of L50. "I wish," writes Mr. Champness in his letter, "I could make you know how much my heart is with you in your great scheme. I am not as sanguine as some of your admirers are as to the success you are sure to win; but I look upon it as a forlorn hope, in which a man had better lose his life than save it by ignoble do-nothingness."

Mrs. Fawcett points out the great value of the Scheme.

MRS. FAWCETT'S VIEWS.

Mrs. Henry Fawcett, lecturing last night on "Private Remedies for Poverty," before the Marylebone Centre of the university Extension Lectures Society, at Welbeck Hall, Welbeck-street, W., said that according to classified directories of London charities, these charities had a yearly income of L4,000,000, but she did not think full returns were made in all instances, and that the total sum was nearer L7,000,000 than L4,000000, while the entire cost of poor-law relief in the United Kingdom was only L8,000,000. Having dwelt upon the evils of misdirected charity, she said the keynote of General Booth's scheme, and what, as it seemed to her, gave her great hope of its being to some extent a success, was the amount of personal devotion and energy which it called for and which she believed the Salvation Army was prepared to give to its development. Its keynote was the possibility of bringing about a change in the individual by personal effort and influence. As General Booth pointed out, the problem was unsolvable unless new soul could be infused in the poor and outcast class whom it was designed to help: and to this end it was not money that was wanted so much as the personal service of men and women. One great feature of the scheme was that no relief was to be given without work, except in very exceptional cases. She had personally visited the workshops and shelters of the Salvation Army in Whitechapel, and she found a number of people apparently of the very lowest moral and physical type, and yet they were de-brutalised and had a happy human look as they went on with their work, which in some cases was the same as they had performed in gaol. No temptation was afforded by the workshops or shelters to induce people to stay away from ordinary industrial life longer than they could possibly help. The men had to sleep in a kind of orange-box without bottom, on the floor, upon an American oilcloth mattress; and with a piece of leather for a coverlet. Most previous schemes for employing the unemployed upon colonies and waste land had failed because of the men put upon them, who were drunken, lazy, and half-witted. By General Booth's scheme there was process of selection which would weed out those individuals: and she thought photography might be employed in getting to know bad and unsatisfactory characters.

Mrs. Howard M'Lean hopes the Scheme may have an immediate trial.

Mrs. Howard M'Lean "presents her compliments to General Booth, and begs to send him her promise of L100, in the earnest hope that the scheme set forth in 'In Darkest England' may at least have a fair trial, and that immediately."

The "Times of India" points out the advantages of the Scheme.

If we apprehend the scheme aright, it will be carried out independently of existing charities, and indeed not under the guise of a charity at all. The bread of poverty is bitter enough, but that of pauperism is bitterer still, and General Booth, it would seem, intends to foster rather than discourage such spirit of independence as he may find among the lost souls for whom he works. But it seems to us that where such a scheme as his chiefly gains its power, is in its total dissociation from church or sect. However good the work which is done by the Church and by the more widely ramified agency of the Non-conformist sects--and no one will be found to deny that this work is of the greatest possible value in relieving the destitute and reclaiming the criminal classes--there is little or no unity about it. It is under no individual control, it is not carried out on any uniform system, and one agency has no means of knowing what another agency is doing. The result is that relief gets very unevenly distributed, and the lazy and dissolute profit at the expense of the deserving poor. Nor do any of these agencies, as a general rule, aim at any system-atic crusade against other destitution than that of the moment. When they touch the lowest of low-life deeps; it is for the most part in the way of temporary relief only, without the effort (because they have not power) to set these people on their feet again and give them the means of earning a living. It is here that General Booth steps in, and by an elaborate but perfectly feasible system, proposes without any attempt at proselytization to drag the poor from their poverty, put them in the way of doing work of any kind they may be fitted for, and eventually establish them in an over-sea colony.

Looking now to the objections which may be urged against General Booth's scheme, we are at once confronted by two important considerations. The first con-cerns the "General" himself. He asks for a million pounds sterling to enable him to carry out his project, and the question seems to have already been asked, Is he the person to whom a million pounds may be entrusted? Will it be so safeguarded that those who subscribe may feel assured that the money will be properly applied and an honest attempt made to do the work here planned out? To all these questions we are disposed to reply in the affirmative. General Booth and his Salvation Army have by this time pretty well weathered the storm of abuse and scorn with which their methods were at first received, and however much we may be disposed even now to question the taste or propriety of those methods, there can be no amount of doubt in the mind of any reasonable man that the Salvation Army has been the means of achieving enormous good the whole world over. In his administration of this huge organization of which himself was the founder, Mr. Booth has proved himself a man of probity and of the strictest possible integrity. We do not hesitate to say that all the money he requires for this great scheme may be safely placed in his hands, and that he will render a strict account of its disbursement. Then comes the question, how far is it possible for him to succeed in the work he proposes to undertake? He has already in the field a vast organization doing good work among the dregs of the population, and the extension of this organization to carry out the main points of his project is not a matter of difficulty. The ill is a terrible one, the evil gigantic, and the means to grapple with it must be gigantic also. But given the means, will they be effective? We frankly confess that we do not believe they will be so effective as General Booth hopes, but we believe at the same time that if he can achieve only one-tenth of what he hopes to achieve, ten millions of pounds would be worthily laid out upon it. The hungry, the dirty, the ragged, the hopeless and outcast, the criminal and the drunkard, the idle and the vicious--can he gather all these in with any hope of starting them afresh on the journey of life? So much work of this kind has already been done without any special system, that there can be little doubt that to a large extent he can. With the honestly poor it is not a difficult matter, but with the vicious and criminal classes, who have no inclination to work so long as they can steal, it will be a long time before the Salvation Army or any other agency can effect any sweeping reform. The work will be slow, but we believe it will be done. It has been objected against General Booth's scheme that it is not new, except in the fact that General Booth proposes that it shall be himself who carries it out. It seems to us, on the contrary, that it is new in one most vital aspect, and that is, that its details are to be worked out by an enormous united body on a definite plan, instead of by numberless charitable agencies all working independently of each other. We believe, in short, that General Booth will meet with a very large measure of success, and we believe also that when the details of his scheme come to be read and discussed, he will have no difficulty in getting all the money he asks for, and more besides. Looking at the enormous wealth of England, a million pounds is as nothing. It is the Duke of Westminister's income for three months, and it would open up the means of finding hope and work and refuge, and a new life beyond the seas, for a million or more of the helpless poor. We wish Mr. Booth God-speed in his great undertaking.

The "Bombay Gazette" of November 15th, 1890, gives an exhaustive review, from which we cull the following extracts:--

There is little of the form, though there may be much of the spirit, of the Salvation Army in General Booth's "Darkest England and the Way Out." It is on the whole a sober, and in some respects well-reasoned, attempt to solve the most urgent problem of the day. Whosesoever the actual workmanship of the book may be, the personality of General Booth pervades every page--nowhere obtrusively it is true, but sufficiently to impart life and warmth to the discussion of a problem whose solution, though it must be sought for only within the limits marked out by economic principles, will never be found, unless it is sought for with a certain passionate sympathy for the outcast. The dramatic parallel which the writer establishes between the savagery of Darkest Africa and the suffering and sin of Darkest England, will arrest attention, and will of itself make the book popular. Here, however, we are concerned with the more matter-of-fact elements in the problem, and with the practical remedies which are proposed for it. The heading of "the Submerged Tenth" which is given to one of the chapters, roughly indicates the dimensions of the task that has to be performed. General Booth takes three millions to be the strength of the army of the destitute in England. The total comprises the representatives of every phase of want--criminals and drunkards and idlers and their dependants, as well as the class who are destitute through misfortune, who are honest in their poverty, and whom no man can blame for it. For these last-named, society does next to nothing. There is the workhouse for people who have spent their last penny; for so long as it remains unspent, it is a legal disqualification for the help of the State. Or there is the casual ward, where a hard task is exacted in payment for hard fare, but where absolutely nothing is done to help the wayfarer to gain or regain a place and a living in society. Out-relief has been reduced to the minimum. A few weeks ago the whole parish of St. Jude, Whitechapel, with a population of sixty thousand, provided only four applicants to the Board of Guardians for out-relief. Thus far the organized official agency has done little enough for the raising of the "submerged tenth." If *laissez faire* were a cure for all the ills of society, they would have been cured long ago, for the remedy has been applied with a persistency that has failed not. General Booth thinks that he has discovered a more excellent way, and is entitled to a hearing for his plan, for part of it is already in operation. In the "shelters" established by the Salvation Army in the east of London, casual relief is given on almost as large a scale as in the casual wards of the London Workhouses; but he claims for it that it is a less degrading form of help, that sympathy goes with it; and with him of course the emotional accompaniments which the Salvation Army is careful to provide, count for much.

The "Christian" prognosticates a good future for the Scheme.

Up to this stage the great social scheme of General Booth for uplifting the "sunken tenth," has been, so to speak, "in the air." Monday night's meeting at Exeter Hall may be said to have set it on the solid ground and given good hope that it will run as fast and as far as the supplied resources will allow. The great audience to which the General had to address himself, was not mainly of the usual enthusiastic Army type; but it cannot be said that it was not ready to approve and applaud when any good and telling point was made. The brief religious service at the beginning gave the proceedings the spiritual stamp of Army gatherings, but the larger part of the time was taken up with the statement of the General. For more than two and a half hours he was on his feet so that he did not, at any rate, spare himself in his effort to interest the public in his gigantic plan of campaign. At the outset, he expressed diffidence in entering on the exposition of somewhat new lines of work, but he soon showed himself at home, and in much that he advanced there was a happy audacity and a confidence that boded well for the future developments of his scheme.

The "Bombay Guardian" defends the Scheme.

General Booth's aim is to give every one who is "down in the world" a chance to rise. No one, however poor or however degraded, is to be left out. By means of shelters and training factories in the towns, he would give every one a chance who wishes to work, however "lost" their character may have become. There is to be absolutely no charity. All will work for their food and lodging, until they have gained sufficient character and experience to take a situation as a respectable working man or woman. There are thousands of "out-of-works," "ne'er-do-wells," &c., in every large town in England, who are naturally fitted for agricultural work, although they have lived all their lives, perhaps, far away from the green fields. For the training of these General Booth has a scheme of a large "Farm Colony" which will be nearly or entirely self-supporting. When trained sufficiently in agricultural work, they will be drafted off by emigration to a great "over-sea" colony in South Africa. The whole movement will be permeated by earnest Christian teaching. The man who is in trouble and professes to be converted, will be welcomed on that account, and the man who is in trouble but does not profess to be saved, will be equally welcome in the hope that he may give himself to Christ.

It is computed that there are three million people in England whom this scheme will eventually hope to help. A first instalment of L100,000 towards an eventual million, is asked for as a starting-point for the scheme.

This seems a large undertaking and a large sum, but compared to the needs of the world, it is very small.

There is a still darker France than the darkest England, a darker Italy than the darkest France, and deeper depths of darkness still in India.

We think that those who know the "slums" of London and large English towns the best, will be the heartiest in wishing God-speed to General Booth's latest movement, which also includes every possible form of Christian benevolent activity.

When Christ reigns as Viceroy for Jehovah for a thousand years, as the Word of God so distinctly intimates, it may be that some such plan as this, far more perfect and world-wide in its aim, will form part of the inaugurative forces of that happy lot.

Speaking broadly, General Booth's great scheme is in harmony with views that are accepted by all Christians. His design is to elevate the wretched to more favourable conditions of life, on the principle of the Temperance reformer who seeks to remove temptations to drunkenness; or of the opponent of the iniquitous opium traffic, who insists upon the prohibition of the drug which is the curse of millions; or of the antagonist of licensed impurity, who demands that the tendency of law shall be to make it easy to do right, and not afford facilities to do wrong. Some passages of "In Darkest England and the Way Out" are certainly capable of being misconstrued. But on looking at the book and its scheme as a whole, the Christian heart is drawn into lively sympathy with it, without being committed to every detail. If all that is anticipated be not realized by this gigantic scheme, the attempt to carry it out cannot do otherwise than prove a source of great and eternal good to multitudes, as the labourers carry on their work in dependance upon God.

The London "Speaker" testifies to the capacity of Gen. Booth for winning the masses.

Seeing from what the Salvation Army has grown, and to what it has grown, we are extremely reluctant to denounce any scheme seriously and carefully elaborated by its leader, as being "too big to be practicable." We must remember who will be the "one head and centre" of the scheme. There are many weak points in General Booth: he is only human. But he is an earnest man; he has proved his talent for organisation; he has proved his capacity for winning the sympathies of the masses. We would say nothing against gentleness, and quiet, and culture. We hope to attain them in the end. It is a pretty work to prune the vine, a beautiful thing to let in the sunlight on the fruit, and to watch the perfection of bloom, and shape, and color; but first of all something has to be done at the roots, something at which we may hold our noses, but which is for all that requisite.

It remains to be seen, first, whether the people concerned would accept the scheme; secondly, whether discipline could be maintained; thirdly, whether money can be raised. As to the first two questions, experience in some degree answers. The people *do* come to the Salvation Army's establishments, and they do behave well in the Shelters and the Workshops. Those who best know the poorer working classes of the country, will be the least likely to despair on these points. A group of poorer English men and women are easily led by a leader who instils regularity and order, and of whose hearty goodwill to them, they are assured. Organisation is in the English blood; and the rougher East End crowd has orderly elements ready to respond at once to the word of command from men and women whom they know and trust. Only the crowd must be sober; and that which its leader preaches must be hope. As to the money, some portion has come in already; and if this is used, as it will be, in making a visible beginning, there will be plenty of people troubled in their consciences who will be ready to give more. Let us give General Booth money, and five years for his experiment. At the end of that time it will be clear enough whether or no the best thing which we can provide for the unemployed is a lethal chamber.

The Book has an unprecedented sale.

Up to the middle of January the book had reached a total circulation of 200,000 copies, beside running through two separate editions in America. It is now being translated into Japanese, French, Swedish and other languages.

The Book of the year.

I do not think I say too much when I say it will not be the attitude ten per cent. after they have read from cover to cover the most remarkable volume that has been issued from the press this year.

A UNIQUE BOOK.

It is a book that stands by itself. In one sense it may be said that there is nothing new in it. That many men are miserable, that it is the duty of all calling themselves

by the name of Christian, to do their utmost to save their perishing brethren, and
that if they set about the task in earnest, certain well-known methods will have
to be resorted to; all this is familiar enough. Neither can it be said that the spirit
of exalted enthusiasm which breathes in every page of the book is one appears for
the first time in the writings of General Booth. It is on the contrary the abiding
evidence of the presence of the Divine Spirit in men, which has never failed in this
world since "the first man stood God conquered, with his face to heaven upturned."
But the unique character of the book arises from the combination of all these elements, with others which have never hitherto been united even within the covers
of a single volume. There is a buoyant enthusiasm in every page, a sanguine optimism at which the youngest among us might marvel, combined with a familiar
acquaintance with the saddest and darkest phenomena of existence. The book deals
with problems which of all others are most calculated to appal, and overwhelm the
minds with the sense of desolation and despair, yet it is instinct throughout with
a joyous hope and glowing confidence. General Booth, face to face with the devil,
still believes in God.

A MIRACLE OF THE BURNING BUSH.

Another distinctive feature of the book is the extent to which it combines the
shrewdest and most practical business capacity with the most exalted religious enthusiasm. The fanatic is usually regarded as somewhat of a fool; no one can read this
book through and think that General Booth has the least deficiency in practical capacity, in shrewd common sense and enormous knowledge of men. From one point
of view it is easy to be a saint, and it is easy to be a man of the world; the difficulty is
to combine the two qualities, the cunning of the serpent with the innocence of the
dove. There is nothing of the naive and guileless innocence of a cloistered virtue in
the book, but though the serpent is very cunning his wiliness and craftiness coexist
with a simple enthusiasm of humanity which is very marvellous to behold. When
we read General Booth's expressions of confidence in the salvability of mankind and
note the intrepid audacity with which he sallies forth like another David to attack
the huge Goliath who threatens the hosts of our modern Israel, and remember that
he is no mere shepherd boy fresh from the fold, but one who for forty years of his
life has lived and laboured in an atmosphere saturated with emanations from every
form of human vice and wretchedness, then we feel somewhat as did Moses when

he stood before the burning bush, "and he looked, and behold the bush burned with fire and the bush was not consumed."

THOMAS CARLYLE REDIVIVUS.

It is impossible not to be impressed by the parallel and at the same time by the contrast between General Booth's book and the latter day prophecies of Mr. Carlyle. For forty years and more Mr. Carlyle prophesied unto the men of his generation, proclaiming in accents of deep earnestness, tinged, however, by a bitter despair, what should be done if we were not utterly to perish. I remember the bitterness with which he told me, while the shadows of the dark valley were gathering round him, that when he wrote his whole soul out in "Latter Day Pamphlets," and delivered to the public that which he believed to be the very truth and inner secret of all things, his message was flouted, and "it was currently reported," said he, with grim resentfulness "it was currently reported that I had written them under the influence of too much whiskey." Now, however, another prophet has arisen with practically the same gospel, but with oh, how different a setting! In Mr. Carlyle's books, his prophetic message shines out lurid as from the background of thundercloud amid the gloom as of an eclipse heralded by portents of ruin and decay. Here "In Darkest England and the Way Out" there is a brightness and a gladness as of a May day sunrise. Infinite hope bubbles up in every page, and in every chapter there is a calm confidence which comes from the experience of one who in sixty years of troubled life can say with full assurance "I know in whom I have believed." That is not the only contrast between the two. Mr. Carlyle as befitted the philosopher in his study, contented himself with writing in large characters of livid fire, "This is the way, walk ye in it;" but the generation scoffed and walked otherwhere. General Booth, equally with Mr. Carlyle writes up in characters so plain that the way-faring man, though a fool, cannot help reading it, "This is the way, walk ye in it." But he does more. He himself offers to lead the van, "This is the way," he declares, "I will lead you along it, follow me!"

CATHOLICITY--SOCIAL AND RELIGIOUS.

Another distinctive characteristic of this book is its extraordinary catholicity. In this respect I know no book like it that has appeared in our time. While declaring with passionate conviction the truth and necessity of the gospel which the Salvation Army preaches, there is not one word of intolerance from the first page to the last. It is easy to be broad when there is no intensity of conviction. The liberality of indifference is one of the most familiar phenomena of the day. But General Booth is broad without being shallow, and his liberalism certainly cannot be attributed to indifference! He is as earnest as John the Baptist, for now and then the aboriginal preacher reappears crying aloud, Jonah-like, messages calling men to flee from the wrath to come. But no broad churchman of our time, from Dean Stanley downwards, could display a more catholic spirit to all fellow workers in the great harvest field, which is white unto the harvest, but where the labourers are so few. This spirit he displays not only in the religious field, but what is still more remarkable, he carries it into the domain of social experiment. The old intolerance and fierce hatred which raged in the churches at many great crises in the history of the world is with us still, but it is no longer in religious dress. The rival sects of socialists hate each other and contend with each other with a savagery which recalls the worst days of the early church. Every man has got his own favourite short cut to Utopia and he damns all those who do not work therein with the unhesitating assurance of an Athanasius. Hence catholicity is much more needed and much more rarely found in the domain of social economics than in that of religious polemices. General Booth as befits a practical man is supremely indifferent to any particular fad, and constructs his scheme on the principle of selecting every proposal which seems to have stuff in it, or is calculated to do any good to suffering humanity. The socialist, the individualist, the political economist, the advocate of emigration, and all social reformers will find what is best in their own particular schemes incorporated in General Booth's schemes. He claims no originality, he disclaims all prejudice even in favour of his own scheme. His suggestions, he says, seem for the moment the most practicable, but he is ready, he tells us with uncompromising frankness, to abandon them to-morrow if any one can show him a better way.

A TEACHABLE PROPHET.

Another extraordinary characteristic of the book is its combination of supreme humility with what the enemy might describe as overweening arrogance. The General's confidence in himself and his men is superb. Not Hildebrand in the height of his power, or Mahommed, at the moment when he was launching the armies which offered to the world Islam or the sword, showed himself more supremely possessed with the confidence of his providential mission than does General Booth in his book. "For this end was I created, to this work was I called, all my life has been a preparation to fit me for its accomplishment." While thus speaking with the confidence of a man who feels himself charged with a divine mission, General Booth displays a humility and a teachableness that is as beautiful as it is rare. Over and over again he deplores his lack of knowledge and the insufficiency of his experience, and admits that his most elaborate proposals may be vitiated by some flaw or some defect which will make itself only too apparent when they get into action. So far from being determined to thrust his scheme as a panacea down the throats of reluctant humanity he appeals to all those who may differ from him not to stand idly cavilling at his proposals, but to produce something better of their own, assuring them that he will be only too good to carry out the best of his ability any scheme which will do more for the benefit of the lapsed classes than his own.

A SHIFTY AND RESOURCEFUL MARINER.

General Booth shows himself in the capacity of a bold and shifty mariner who has been ordered to take a ship filled with precious cargo across a stormy and rock-strewn ocean to a distant port. Quicksands abound, cross currents continually threaten to carry the ship from her course, the wind shifts from point to point, now rising to a hurricane and then dying away to a dead calm. But alike by night and day, whether the sky be black with clouds, or bright with radiant sunshine, in the teeth of the wind or in a favourable gale, he presses forward to his distant haven. He will tack to the right or to the left, availing himself to the utmost of every favourable current and every passing breeze, supremely indifferent to all accusations of inconsistency, or of deviating from the straight line from the port which he left to the port for which he is bound, if so he can get the quicker and the more safely to his goal. Hitherto General Booth had practically been in the condition of a Captain who relied solely on his boilers to make his voyage. "Get up steam, make the heart right, keep the furnace fires going, and drive ahead through the darkness regardless of a lowering tempest or of the swift rushing current which sweeps you from your course." This book proclaims his decision in favour of adopting a less reckless and more practical mode of navigation. While his reliance is still placed on the inner central fire he will not disdain to utilise the currents, the tides, and the winds which will make it easier for his straining boilers and untiring screw to forge its way across the sea.

The book is interesting in itself as a book, but of the bookmaking part of it, it is absurd to speak. You might as well speak of the rivets and the paint, in describing the performance of a Cunarder; as to speak of the literary merits or demerits of this book. As a piece of actuality, full of life and force, it comes to us in paper and ink and between two covers; but the vehicle of its presentation is as indifferent as the quality of the boards in which it is bound. The supreme thing is not the form but the substance.--The Review of Reviews.

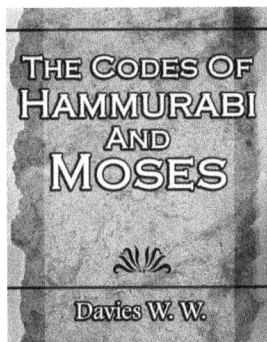

The Codes Of Hammurabi And Moses
W. W. Davies

QTY

The discovery of the Hammurabi Code is one of the greatest achievements of archaeology, and is of paramount interest, not only to the student of the Bible, but also to all those interested in ancient history...

Religion   **ISBN:** *1-59462-338-4*

Pages:132
MSRP $12.95

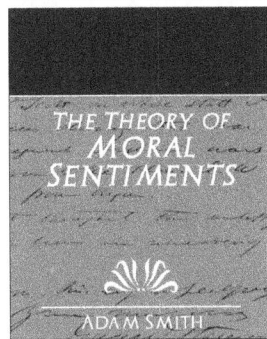

The Theory of Moral Sentiments
Adam Smith

QTY

This work from 1749. contains original theories of conscience amd moral judgment and it is the foundation for systemof morals.

Philosophy **ISBN:** *1-59462-777-0*

Pages:536
MSRP $19.95

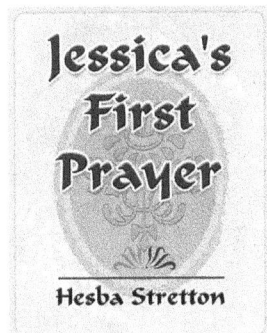

Jessica's First Prayer
Hesba Stretton

QTY

In a screened and secluded corner of one of the many railway-bridges which span the streets of London there could be seen a few years ago, from five o'clock every morning until half past eight, a tidily set-out coffee-stall, consisting of a trestle and board, upon which stood two large tin cans, with a small fire of charcoal burning under each so as to keep the coffee boiling during the early hours of the morning when the work-people were thronging into the city on their way to their daily toil...

Pages:84

Childrens   **ISBN:** *1-59462-373-2*

MSRP $9.95

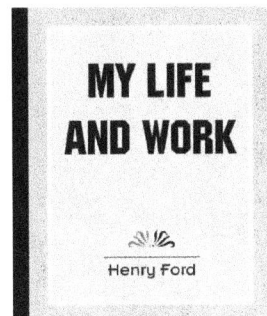

My Life and Work
Henry Ford

QTY

Henry Ford revolutionized the world with his implementation of mass production for the Model T automobile. Gain valuable business insight into his life and work with his own auto-biography... "We have only started on our development of our country we have not as yet, with all our talk of wonderful progress, done more than scratch the surface. The progress has been wonderful enough but..."

Pages:300

Biographies/   **ISBN:** *1-59462-198-5*

MSRP $21.95

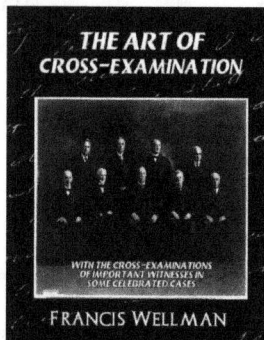

The Art of Cross-Examination
Francis Wellman

QTY

I presume it is the experience of every author, after his first book is published upon an important subject, to be almost overwhelmed with a wealth of ideas and illustrations which could readily have been included in his book, and which to his own mind, at least, seem to make a second edition inevitable. Such certainly was the case with me; and when the first edition had reached its sixth impression in five months, I rejoiced to learn that it seemed to my publishers that the book had met with a sufficiently favorable reception to justify a second and considerably enlarged edition. ..

Reference **ISBN:** *1-59462-647-2*

Pages:412
MSRP $19.95

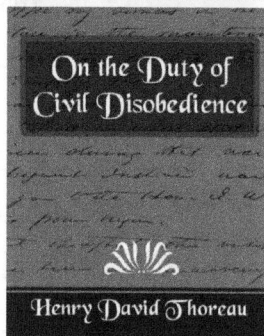

On the Duty of Civil Disobedience
Henry David Thoreau

QTY

Thoreau wrote his famous essay, On the Duty of Civil Disobedience, as a protest against an unjust but popular war and the immoral but popular institution of slave-owning. He did more than write—he declined to pay his taxes, and was hauled off to gaol in consequence. Who can say how much this refusal of his hastened the end of the war and of slavery ?

Law **ISBN:** *1-59462-747-9*

Pages:48
MSRP $7.45

Dream Psychology Psychoanalysis for Beginners
Sigmund Freud

QTY

Sigmund Freud, born Sigismund Schlomo Freud (May 6, 1856 - September 23, 1939), was a Jewish-Austrian neurologist and psychiatrist who co-founded the psychoanalytic school of psychology. Freud is best known for his theories of the unconscious mind, especially involving the mechanism of repression; his redefinition of sexual desire as mobile and directed towards a wide variety of objects; and his therapeutic techniques, especially his understanding of transference in the therapeutic relationship and the presumed value of dreams as sources of insight into unconscious desires.

Psychology **ISBN:** *1-59462-905-6*

Pages:196
MSRP $15.45

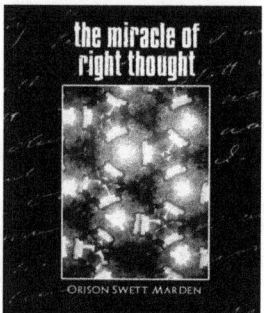

The Miracle of Right Thought
Orison Swett Marden

QTY

Believe with all of your heart that you will do what you were made to do. When the mind has once formed the habit of holding cheerful, happy, prosperous pictures, it will not be easy to form the opposite habit. It does not matter how improbable or how far away this realization may see, or how dark the prospects may be, if we visualize them as best we can, as vividly as possible, hold tenaciously to them and vigorously struggle to attain them, they will gradually become actualized, realized in the life. But a desire, a longing without endeavor, a yearning abandoned or held indifferently will vanish without realization.

Self Help **ISBN:** *1-59462-644-8*

Pages:360
MSRP $25.45

The Rosicrucian Cosmo-Conception Mystic Christianity by *Max Heindel*   ISBN: *1-59462-188-8*   **$38.95**
The Rosicrucian Cosmo-conception is not dogmatic, neither does it appeal to any other authority than the reason of the student. It is: not controversial, but is: sent forth in the, hope that it may help to clear...   New Age/Religion Pages 646

Abandonment To Divine Providence by *Jean-Pierre de Caussade*   ISBN: *1-59462-228-0*   **$25.95**
"The Rev. Jean Pierre de Caussade was one of the most remarkable spiritual writers of the Society of Jesus in France in the 18th Century. His death took place at Toulouse in 1751. His works have gone through many editions and have been republished...   Inspirational/Religion Pages 400

Mental Chemistry by *Charles Haanel*   ISBN: *1-59462-192-6*   **$23.95**
Mental Chemistry allows the change of material conditions by combining and appropriately utilizing the power of the mind. Much like applied chemistry creates something new and unique out of careful combinations of chemicals the mastery of mental chemistry...   New Age Pages 354

The Letters of Robert Browning and Elizabeth Barret Barrett 1845-1846 vol II   ISBN: *1-59462-193-4*   **$35.95**
by *Robert Browning* and *Elizabeth Barrett*   Biographies Pages 596

Gleanings In Genesis (volume I) by *Arthur W. Pink*   ISBN: *1-59462-130-6*   **$27.45**
Appropriately has Genesis been termed "the seed plot of the Bible" for in it we have, in germ form, almost all of the great doctrines which are afterwards fully developed in the books of Scripture which follow...   Religion/Inspirational Pages 420

The Master Key by *L. W. de Laurence*   ISBN: *1-59462-001-6*   **$30.95**
In no branch of human knowledge has there been a more lively increase of the spirit of research during the past few years than in the study of Psychology, Concentration and Mental Discipline. The requests for authentic lessons in Thought Control, Mental Discipline and...   New Age/Business Pages 422

The Lesser Key Of Solomon Goetia by *L. W. de Laurence*   ISBN: *1-59462-092-X*   **$9.95**
This translation of the first book of the "Lemegton" which is now for the first time made accessible to students of Talismanic Magic was done, after careful collation and edition, from numerous Ancient Manuscripts in Hebrew, Latin, and French...   New Age/Occult Pages 92

Rubaiyat Of Omar Khayyam by *Edward Fitzgerald*   ISBN:*1-59462-332-5*   **$13.95**
Edward Fitzgerald, whom the world has already learned, in spite of his own efforts to remain within the shadow of anonymity, to look upon as one of the rarest poets of the century, was born at Bredfield, in Suffolk, on the 31st of March, 1809. He was the third son of John Purcell...   Music Pages 172

Ancient Law by *Henry Maine*   ISBN: *1-59462-128-4*   **$29.95**
The chief object of the following pages is to indicate some of the earliest ideas of mankind, as they are reflected in Ancient Law, and to point out the relation of those ideas to modern thought.   Religion/History Pages 452

Far-Away Stories by *William J. Locke*   ISBN: *1-59462-129-2*   **$19.45**
"Good wine needs no bush, but a collection of mixed vintages does. And this book is just such a collection. Some of the stories I do not want to remain buried for ever in the museum files of dead magazine-numbers an author's not unpardonable vanity..."   Fiction Pages 272

Life of David Crockett by *David Crockett*   ISBN: *1-59462-250-7*   **$27.45**
"Colonel David Crockett was one of the most remarkable men of the times in which he lived. Born in humble life, but gifted with a strong will, an indomitable courage, and unremitting perseverance...   Biographies/New Age Pages 424

Lip-Reading by *Edward Nitchie*   ISBN: *1-59462-206-X*   **$25.95**
Edward B. Nitchie, founder of the New York School for the Hard of Hearing, now the Nitchie School of Lip-Reading, Inc, wrote "LIP-READING Principles and Practice". The development and perfecting of this meritorious work on lip-reading was an undertaking...   How-to Pages 400

A Handbook of Suggestive Therapeutics, Applied Hypnotism, Psychic Science   ISBN: *1-59462-214-0*   **$24.95**
by *Henry Munro*   Health/New Age/Health/Self-help Pages 376

A Doll's House: and Two Other Plays by *Henrik Ibsen*   ISBN: *1-59462-112-8*   **$19.95**
Henrik Ibsen created this classic when in revolutionary 1848 Rome. Introducing some striking concepts in playwriting for the realist genre, this play has been studied the world over.   Fiction/Classics/Plays 308

The Light of Asia by *sir Edwin Arnold*   ISBN: *1-59462-204-3*   **$13.95**
In this poetic masterpiece, Edwin Arnold describes the life and teachings of Buddha. The man who was to become known as Buddha to the world was born as Prince Gautama of India but he rejected the worldly riches and abandoned the reigns of power when...   Religion/History/Biographies Pages 170

The Complete Works of Guy de Maupassant by *Guy de Maupassant*   ISBN: *1-59462-157-8*   **$16.95**
"For days and days, nights and nights, I had dreamed of that first kiss which was to consecrate our engagement, and I knew not on what spot I should put my lips..."   Fiction/Classics Pages 240

The Art of Cross-Examination by *Francis L. Wellman*   ISBN: *1-59462-309-0*   **$26.95**
Written by a renowned trial lawyer, Wellman imparts his experience and uses case studies to explain how to use psychology to extract desired information through questioning.   How-to/Science/Reference Pages 408

Answered or Unanswered? by *Louisa Vaughan*   ISBN: *1-59462-248-5*   **$10.95**
Miracles of Faith in China   Religion Pages 112

The Edinburgh Lectures on Mental Science (1909) by *Thomas*   ISBN: *1-59462-008-3*   **$11.95**
This book contains the substance of a course of lectures recently given by the writer in the Queen Street Hall, Edinburgh. Its purpose is to indicate the Natural Principles governing the relation between Mental Action and Material Conditions...   New Age/Psychology Pages 148

Ayesha by *H. Rider Haggard*   ISBN: *1-59462-301-5*   **$24.95**
Verily and indeed it is the unexpected that happens! Probably if there was one person upon the earth from whom the Editor of this, and of a certain previous history, did not expect to hear again...   Classics Pages 380

Ayala's Angel by *Anthony Trollope*   ISBN: *1-59462-352-X*   **$29.95**
The two girls were both pretty, but Lucy who was twenty-one who supposed to be simple and comparatively unattractive, whereas Ayala was credited, as her Bombwhat romantic name might show, with poetic charm and a taste for romance. Ayala when her father died was nineteen...   Fiction Pages 484

The American Commonwealth by *James Bryce*   ISBN: *1-59462-286-8*   **$34.45**
An interpretation of American democratic political theory. It examines political mechanics and society from the perspective of Scotsman James Bryce   Politics Pages 572

Stories of the Pilgrims by *Margaret P. Pumphrey*   ISBN: *1-59462-116-0*   **$17.95**
This book explores pilgrims religious oppression in England as well as their escape to Holland and eventual crossing to America on the Mayflower, and their early days in New England...   History Pages 268

QTY

The Fasting Cure *by Sinclair Upton*   ISBN: *1-59462-222-1* **$13.95**
In the Cosmopolitan Magazine for May, 1910, and in the Contemporary Review (London) for April, 1910, I published an article dealing with my experiences in fasting. I have written a great many magazine articles, but never one which attracted so much attention... New Age/Self Help/Health Pages 164

Hebrew Astrology *by Sepharial*   ISBN: *1-59462-308-2* **$13.45**
In these days of advanced thinking it is a matter of common observation that we have left many of the old landmarks behind and that we are now pressing forward to greater heights and to a wider horizon than that which represented the mind-content of our progenitors...   Astrology Pages 144

Thought Vibration or The Law of Attraction in the Thought World   ISBN: *1-59462-127-6* **$12.95**
by William Walker Atkinson   *Psychology/Religion Pages 144*

Optimism *by Helen Keller*   ISBN: *1-59462-108-X* **$15.95**
Helen Keller was blind, deaf, and mute since 19 months old, yet famously learned how to overcome these handicaps, communicate with the world, and spread her lectures promoting optimism. An inspiring read for everyone...   Biographies/Inspirational Pages 84

Sara Crewe *by Frances Burnett*   ISBN: *1-59462-360-0* **$9.45**
In the first place, Miss Minchin lived in London. Her home was a large, dull, tall one, in a large, dull square, where all the houses were alike, and all the sparrows were alike, and where all the door-knockers made the same heavy sound...   Childrens/Classic Pages 88

The Autobiography of Benjamin Franklin *by Benjamin Franklin*   ISBN: *1-59462-135-7* **$24.95**
The Autobiography of Benjamin Franklin has probably been more extensively read than any other American historical work, and no other book of its kind has had such ups and downs of fortune. Franklin lived for many years in England, where he was agent...   Biographies/History Pages 332

Name	
Email	
Telephone	
Address	
City, State ZIP	

☐ **Credit Card**   ☐ **Check / Money Order**

Credit Card Number	
Expiration Date	
Signature	

Please Mail to: Book Jungle
PO Box 2226
Champaign, IL 61825
or Fax to: 630-214-0564

ORDERING INFORMATION

web: *www.bookjungle.com*
email: *sales@bookjungle.com*
fax: *630-214-0564*
mail: *Book Jungle PO Box 2226 Champaign, IL 61825*
or PayPal *to sales@bookjungle.com*

Please contact us for bulk discounts

DIRECT-ORDER TERMS

**20% Discount if You Order
Two or More Books**
Free Domestic Shipping!
Accepted: Master Card, Visa,
Discover, American Express

www.ingramcontent.com/pod-product-compliance
Lightning Source LLC
Chambersburg PA
CBHW080532090426

42733CB00015B/2560